Letizia Battaglia

Introduction by Walter Guadagnini

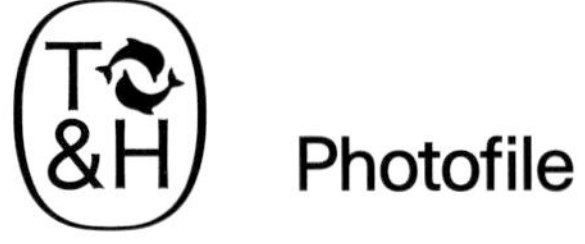

Photofile

Anger and Joy

Trying to rebuild her life away from her beloved Palermo, at
thirty-six years old, with two of her daughters, a new partner – the
photographer Santi Caleca – and a camera given to her by a friend: so
began, between Sicily and Milan, almost from scratch, the career of
one of the most famous photojournalists of the late twentieth century,
honoured with the W. Eugene Smith Grant in 1985 and celebrated in
countless exhibitions in her lifetime and especially after her death
in 2022. A career that was in some ways anomalous (it started late,
after all, and there was nothing in her life to suggest the youthful
passion for photography so common in photographers' anecdotes),
it began as a corollary to written journalism, which appeared to be
Battaglia's true vocation.

In Milan, in the early 1970s, in the midst of a period still
responding to the awakening of 1968 and its myriad visions of utopia,
Letizia Battaglia wrote for a few offbeat magazines that combined
investigative journalism with erotic entertainment. Her work merged
support for the great civil struggles of the time (above all the battle
for the right to divorce, which would culminate in the historic
1974 referendum, whose result signalled the opening up of Italian
society to modern ways still unacceptable to the Church and its
political wing, the Democrazia Cristiana) with hints at a sexuality
still experienced in the context of a deeply rooted male chauvinist
culture, which began to show its first cracks with the spread of
an increasingly aware and assertive feminism. In these social and
journalistic circumstances, Battaglia produced articles on a wide
range of topics, from prostitution to the gay community's meeting
places (subjects that were still taboo for the mainstream press of the
time), from the use of the contraceptive pill by underage girls to the
daily lives of those on military service, using a language that was
direct and immediate, polemical and passionate, sometimes witty.
In later years, these would be the principal characteristics that would
inform her photographic practice. And it was on the pages of those
magazines, alongside stock images sourced by the editorial staff,

that her first photographs were published, accompanying her articles. These were mainly nudes, *mises en scène* of situations reflecting the content of the articles, but attracting the reader's attention with voyeuristic tones whose innocence, in retrospect, prompts a smile. At this time, Letizia Battaglia had no creative intent; this was simply her professional practice, developed alongside her partner who was also her first photography teacher. Yet on these pages and in these images there was a focus on the body, especially the female body, and its potential ability to offer freedom from the constraints of middle-class society, from which Battaglia herself had only recently escaped. This focus would return as a constant in her later work, less tied to the news and with a more creative slant. Perhaps it is no coincidence that her final images were female nudes, testifying to an abiding source of inspiration that extended over and persisted through the tragic times of news photography, like a hymn to life expressed through the female body.

This period did not last long, however, and by the mid-1970s Letizia Battaglia was back in Sicily's regional capital, about to become involved in a very different type of journalism and photography. She was hired to cover news in Palermo by the daily paper *L'Ora* – where she had published her very first photos in 1969 – a newspaper that took an explicit stand against the Mafia and its political and economic connections, as against the more institutional and widely read *Giornale di Sicilia*. Together with Santi Caleca and then with her new partner Franco Zecchin, another fundamental figure in both her private and professional life – the two aspects were and always would be indissolubly linked for Letizia Battaglia – she very quickly found herself leading a team of photographers destined to figure not only in the history of photography but also in the history of contemporary Italian society, as able and courageous witnesses to one of the most dramatic periods for Sicily and the Republic of Italy. This was the time of the Mafia wars, fought between the mid-1970s and the early 1990s, when the double murder of judges Falcone and Borsellino marked a culmination of provocations to the State that would lead Letizia Battaglia to give up news photography, overwhelmed by the horror and the powerlessness. We should not forget, however, that

before then, in the late 1980s, Battaglia had left the newspaper and
put her political passion into practice, first as a successful candidate
for the city council elections – where she was appointed to a lead
role in mayor Leoluca Orlando's reforming council – and later as a
regional deputy: a pathway that shows on one hand the multiplicity
of her interests and on the other the coherence of her ideas and her
ability to turn them into reality.

News photography, then, with the emphasis on devastating
news filled with violence and murders, literally featuring blood and
tears, the blood of the victims and the tears of those left behind;
photography that could make no distinction between those who
were good and those who were bad, even though it was clear which
were which, and those who stood in the middle – and there were
many of these, especially in the political classes; photography that
was required to show the results of the shootings and ambushes,
uncensored, without deception, the raw truth. In only one
instance, perhaps, did Letizia Battaglia shy away from exposing
and spotlighting the city's dark side, something that was for her a
moral duty: the moment of Boris Giuliano's death. Giuliano was the
police chief who headed up Palermo's Mobile Squad and Battaglia
had a particularly strong attachment to him: she said that it was he
who had allowed her to move forward through the crowd clustered
around a corpse, giving her legitimacy – when she was still young and
relatively unknown – in two worlds, the forces of order and the world
of photographers, both still steeped in a macho culture. But Giuliano
was above all a representative of the State whose moral rectitude
made him admired and respected even by the criminal fraternity.
On that occasion, Battaglia created a sort of *vanitas*, a still life with a
bunch of roses resting on the victim's desk, an image with a strong
symbolic charge. As though, in the middle of all the screams and
gunshots, she felt the need for a moment of silence.

However, this instance is not the key to Battaglia's photography
of the Mafia and its carnage, because her photography was always
activist, denouncing and documenting, bearing witness. This is partly
what sets her photography apart from the potential comparisons
offered by the medium's history, above all the photographer who

seems to be her most direct antecedent, Weegee. He never made room for explicit activism, nor did he ever aspire to awaken New York consciences, because he operated in a very different social and political context. Weegee was in his own right engaged in social issues and held two famous exhibitions at the Photo League, under the ironic title 'Murder Is My Business'. However, although these did show the poverty-related tragedies of New York, it was within a cultural space and with the detachment of a reporter. Letizia Battaglia and the photographers working for *L'Ora* in the 'Photographic News' department, on the other hand, mounted an exhibition in the streets of Palermo and of Corleone, erecting panels in public spaces that were direct denunciations of the Mafia and direct invitations to the public to wake up to the situation's extreme drama and unsustainability. This was reportage certainly, but also activism.

In the same way, Battaglia never undertook true long-term projects on specific themes, unlike other photographers who were close to her either in date or conceptually, such as Susan Meiselas, Josef Koudelka, Donna Ferrato and Sebastião Salgado. She never transformed her photojournalism into something else, something considered and systematically ordered: she left it to the photographs themselves, taken at different times and in different circumstances, to construct their own intelligible story with a unified narrative that transcended individual events. And looking across all of Letizia Battaglia's production from the mid-1970s to the early 2000s, it is also true to say that something which might be a sort of design, hidden but not accidental, is slowly revealed through these decades of photography: a great tableau of her native land, extending from Palermo right across Sicily. This is how the big picture is completed: never made explicit but fulfilled in tangible terms.

It is for this reason that Battaglia, especially in her later years, strongly opposed the description of 'Mafia photographer', a label applied to her both at home and abroad, as labels often are to those who become famous. In the final analysis, her shots of murders, corpses, arrests and of the personalities linked to that world, some well known, some less so, are only a part – and not even the most numerous part – of those she took in Sicily over the years. In fact, she created a true *comédie humaine* which, alongside the tragic, also shows the lyrical, the comical and the whole range of emotions and feelings that it is possible to experience when considering human beings, their behaviour and their lives.

On closer examination, all of Letizia Battaglia's work is characterized by a coexistence – which must not be mistaken for a coincidence – of opposites, manifested in its most basic, one might almost say primordial sense, in her almost exclusive preference for black and white. This lies at the root of nearly all her images, from the extraordinary portrait of Rosaria Schifani to 'The little girl and the darkness', in which the composition is brought to life by the contrast between light and shadow, between the visible, sunny part and the invisible, nocturnal part, in a dichotomy as fundamental as it is effective in terms of communication. Then again, it is impossible not to think about the pairing of poverty and wealth, which has a particular presence in the photographs of the second half of the 1970s, when *L'Ora*'s crusading work was mostly concentrated on laying bare the desperate living conditions in many parts of Palermo, both in the centre and on the outskirts. In this case too, the more gritty and direct photographs alternate with those that are more symbolic in nature, as seen in the bitter irony of the image of a rat and a cat so sated with food waste that they have even forgotten their proverbial hatred for one another. And still on the subject of animals, this time in connection with wealth, there is a searing wit in another title: 'Aristocratic garden reception with dead fox', in which Battaglia's typical close-up view (in this sense, she was heir to Robert Capa and his assertion that 'if your pictures aren't good enough, you're not close enough') becomes a tool to mock not just a single individual but the whole class of people that the subject represents.

It is clear, nonetheless, that this image is one of Letizia Battaglia's great portraits, a genre that has yielded some of her best examples. Whether posed or candid, the faces she portrays are always a sort of affirmation of identity, of uniqueness: they stand out from the crowd precisely because they are individual, telling a whole story, as in the gallery of her best-known subjects, very young and adolescent girls. In these, Battaglia essentially created a sort of *a posteriori* self-portrait, almost as though she were trying to rediscover the dreams and hopes that had disappeared from her life too quickly – although they were rediscovered in later years, albeit tinged with a rage that was as much social as it was personal, never abating, but instead becoming a stimulus for action, both public and private ('We still have the beautiful experience of carrying forward and sharing our anger and our joy', she said). But equally, we must not overlook her crowd scenes, since her photography was destined to provide an account of an entire land through its inhabitants: whether they were rallies or processions, celebrations or protests, crowds were an important part of her explorations. Perhaps her most accomplished images were those shot during religious festivals, when groups of people seemed to be filled with a sort of uncontrollable energy, a potentially overwhelming wave, even though in reality this was governed by a series of rituals through which these events helped to define a society's identity, originating in ancient times and still far from dying out. In this series too, there is an image that assumes an almost metaphorical quality: the photograph of a dove that seems to be aiming directly at the faces of two children watching it, a symbol of peace involuntarily transformed, for a moment, into a potentially blunt instrument. A reversal of traditional expectations, and at the same time a metaphor for Battaglia's photography itself, ready to capture in a single image life in all its most diverse and even extreme aspects, which become meaningful and worth photographing precisely because they represent a break in the continuity of existence – not necessarily an unusual one – in which there is a concentration of beauty that comes primarily from emotion.

From this point onwards, it is not difficult to follow Letizia Battaglia on her journey towards a vision of the world through photography, where the alternation of joy and suffering, for example, becomes a crucial element in the narrative, in the very experience of being in the world. How many faces and bodies express these two feelings, making them among the most striking of all those that Battaglia photographed? We are immediately reminded of the patients confined in the psychiatric hospital where Battaglia's main role was to run theatre workshops (once again in partnership with Zecchin), in other words working not primarily as a photographer but as someone who was socially committed. This provides still more evidence that it was the circumstances of her life – mainly but not exclusively her public life – that drove Letizia Battaglia to produce her photographs. In addition to her commitments in the worlds of politics and journalism, this also explains her perseverance in fulfilling her dream to establish the Centro Internazionale di Fotografia at the Cantieri Culturali alla Zisa in Palermo – not as a place to celebrate her own work, but somewhere where photography could connect with the city and become an integral part of its cultural fabric. Yet another example of activism through photography, this time viewed more as a collective language than as the work of an individual.

There is a suffering that passes over sequestered bodies and through eyes that are lost in the void or gaze inquisitively into the camera. This is different but certainly no less than that experienced by the family of someone who has died, such as the child watching over his father's corpse in an image of rare compositional complexity for a photographer like Battaglia, who handled space in an extremely condensed manner. In this respect, it is enough to look at the scenes containing murder victims to understand the theatricality of the space constructed by Battaglia's lens: streets, courtyards, rural settings and apartments all become stage sets for tragedies repeated a thousand times – this was the number of victims of the Mafia in Palermo and its province in the first five years of the 1980s – always unfolding differently but always with the same ending.

However, alongside the depiction of suffering, joy also appears with equal regularity, in scenes that are truly breathtaking. A kiss in the countryside or on a beach, a child thrown in the air during a festival, the quiet contentment of two women knitting on Easter Monday or boys playing football – these are always the other side of the coin, revealing a vision of the world, not only of photography, a thirst for life that found a way to take concrete shape in photography.

Here we must let the photographer speak for herself: 'It was life I sought, death was an event I wasn't looking for, I was required to take photographs and so I did. What I did of my own free will

was to mount exhibitions against the Mafia on the street, but
I photographed crime because the newspaper sent me to do it.
And that was a good thing. For my part, I have always looked for life:
so many photographs of people expressing love, hugging and kissing,
little girls and little boys, couples, wonderful old women.' As if, to be
complete, this story of life had to contain death too, even though it
wasn't looked for, because that is how life is.

Walter Guadagnini

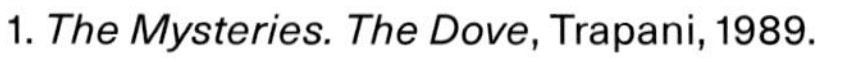

1. *The Mysteries. The Dove*, Trapani, 1989.

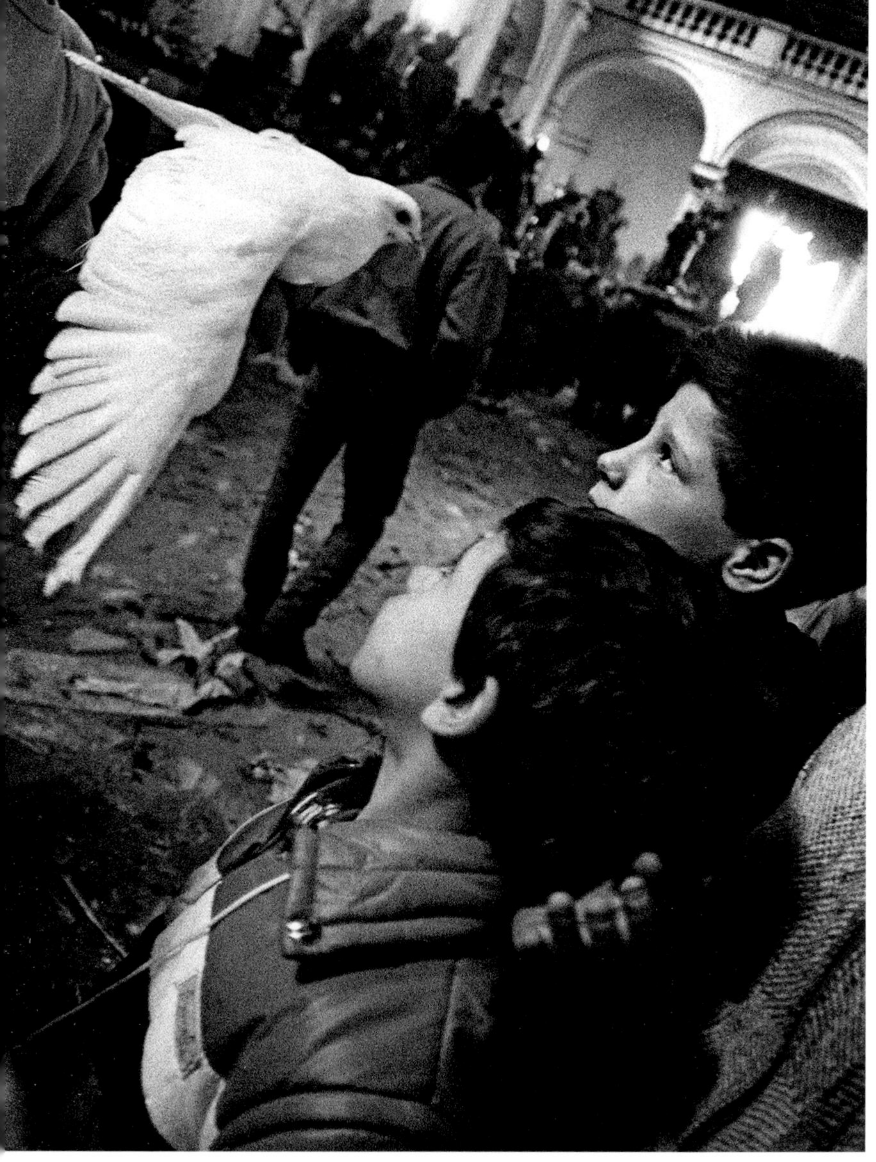

2. Palermo, 1984.

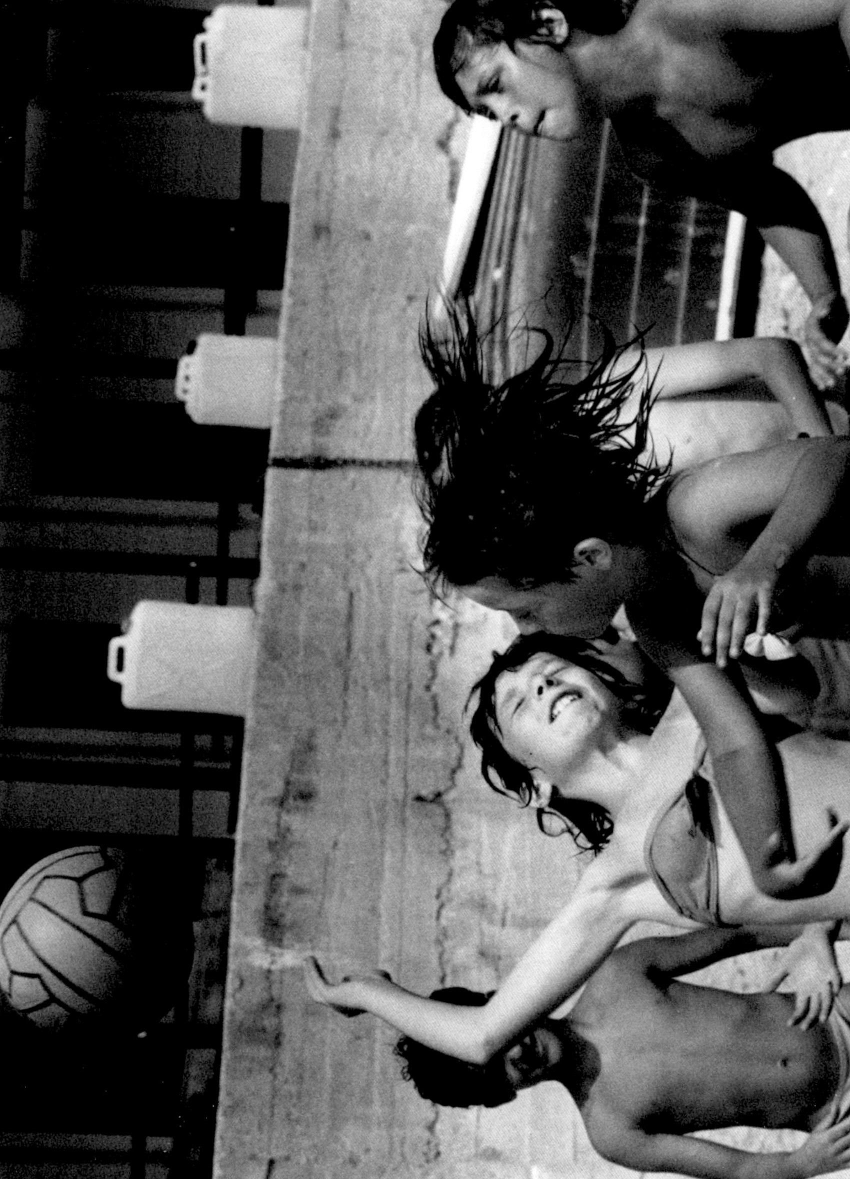

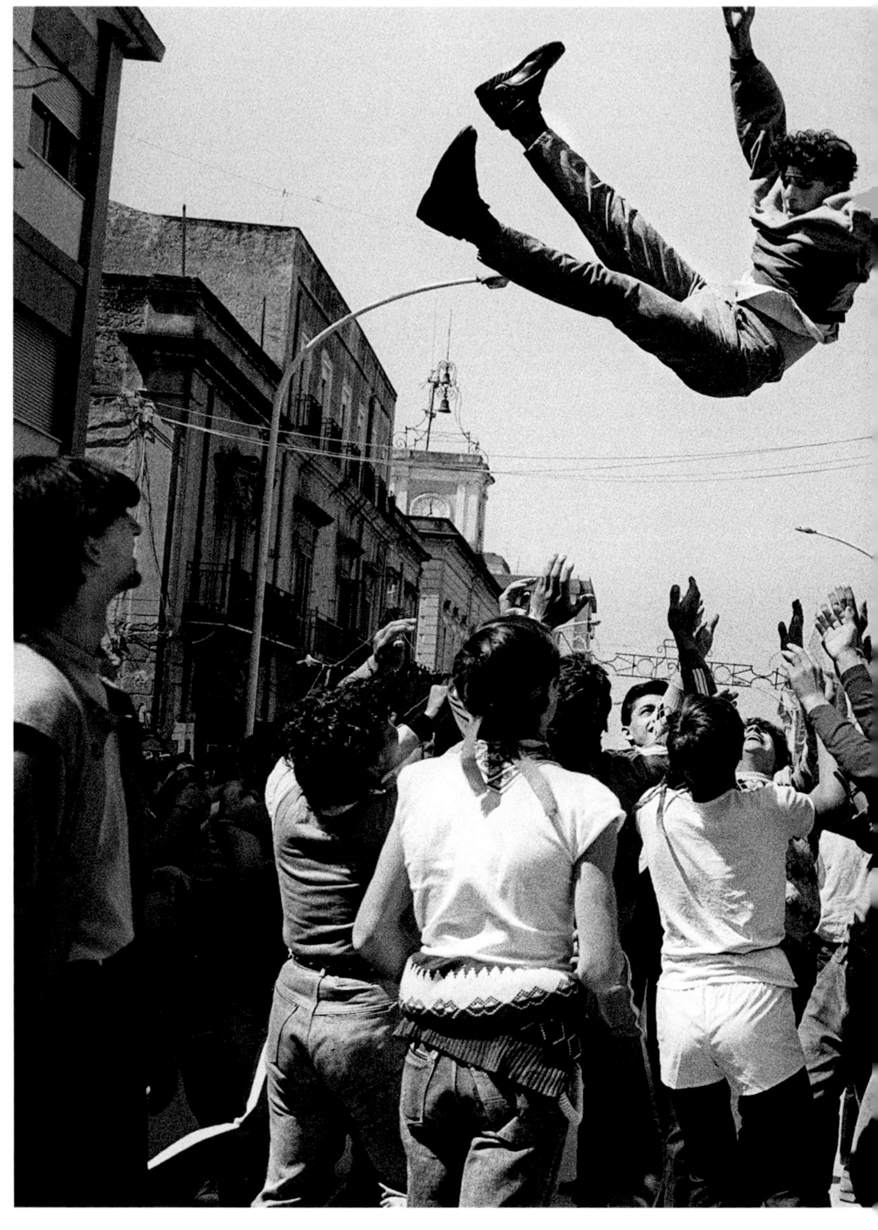

3. *Easter Sunday. 'Largo, largo' festival*, Ribera, 1984.

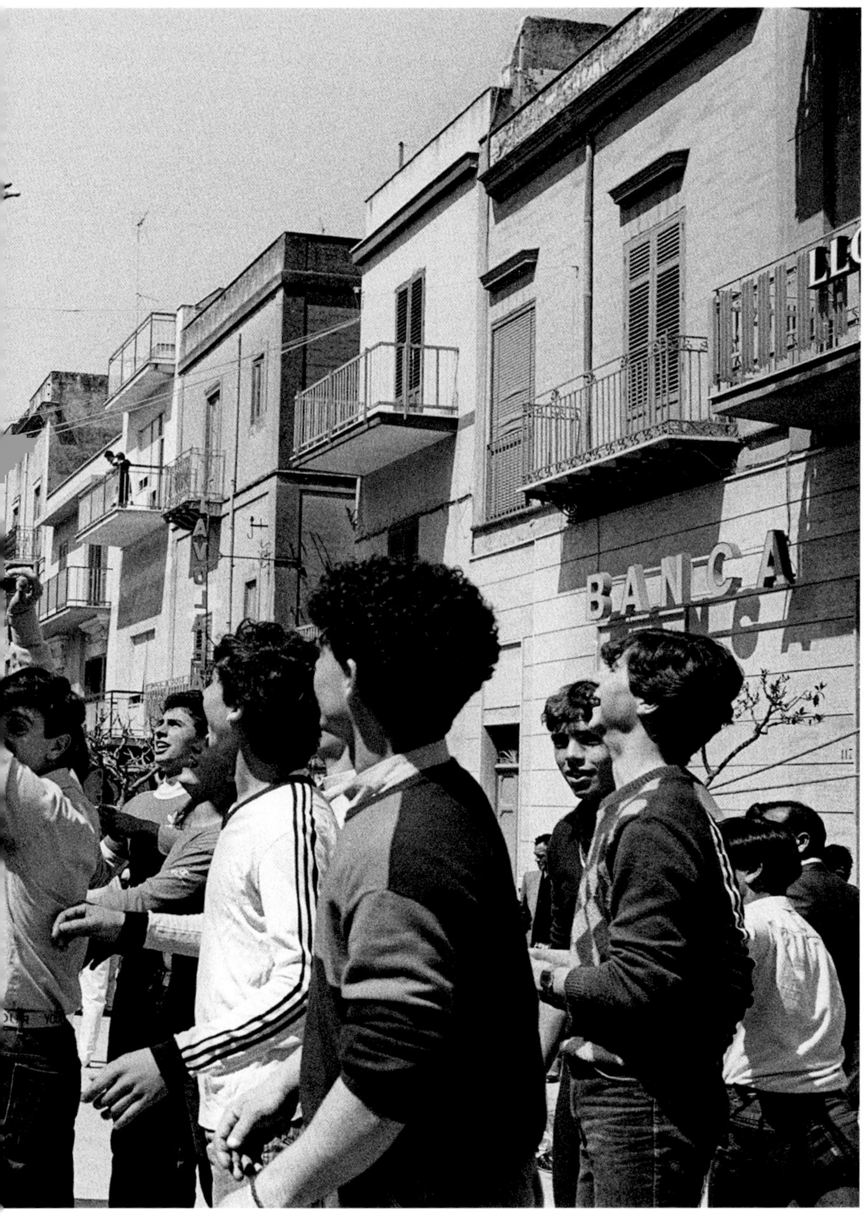

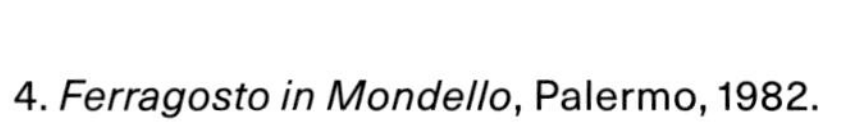

4. *Ferragosto in Mondello*, Palermo, 1982.

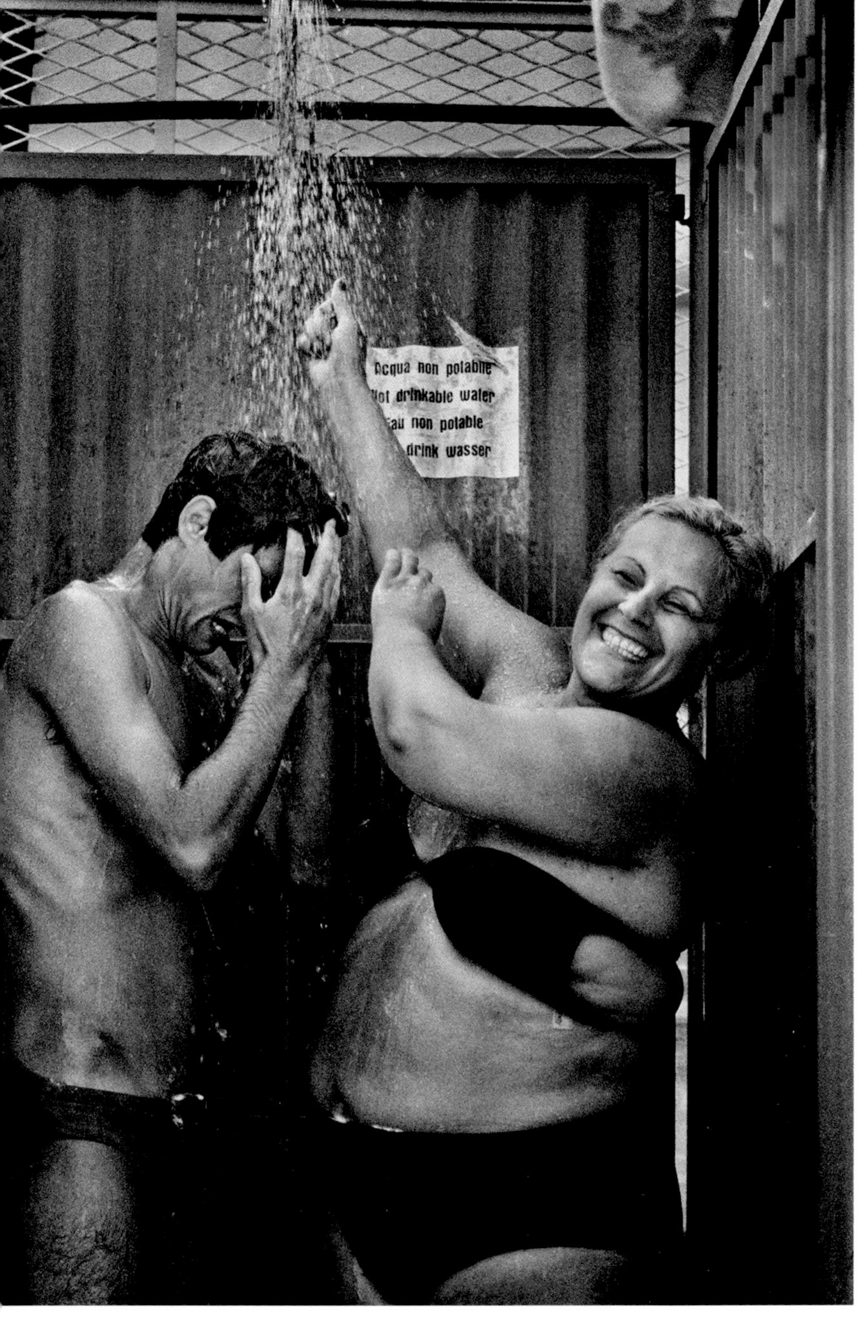
Acqua non potabile
Not drinkable water
Eau non potable
drink wasser

5. *Sabina and Pippo in love*, Prizzi, 1983.

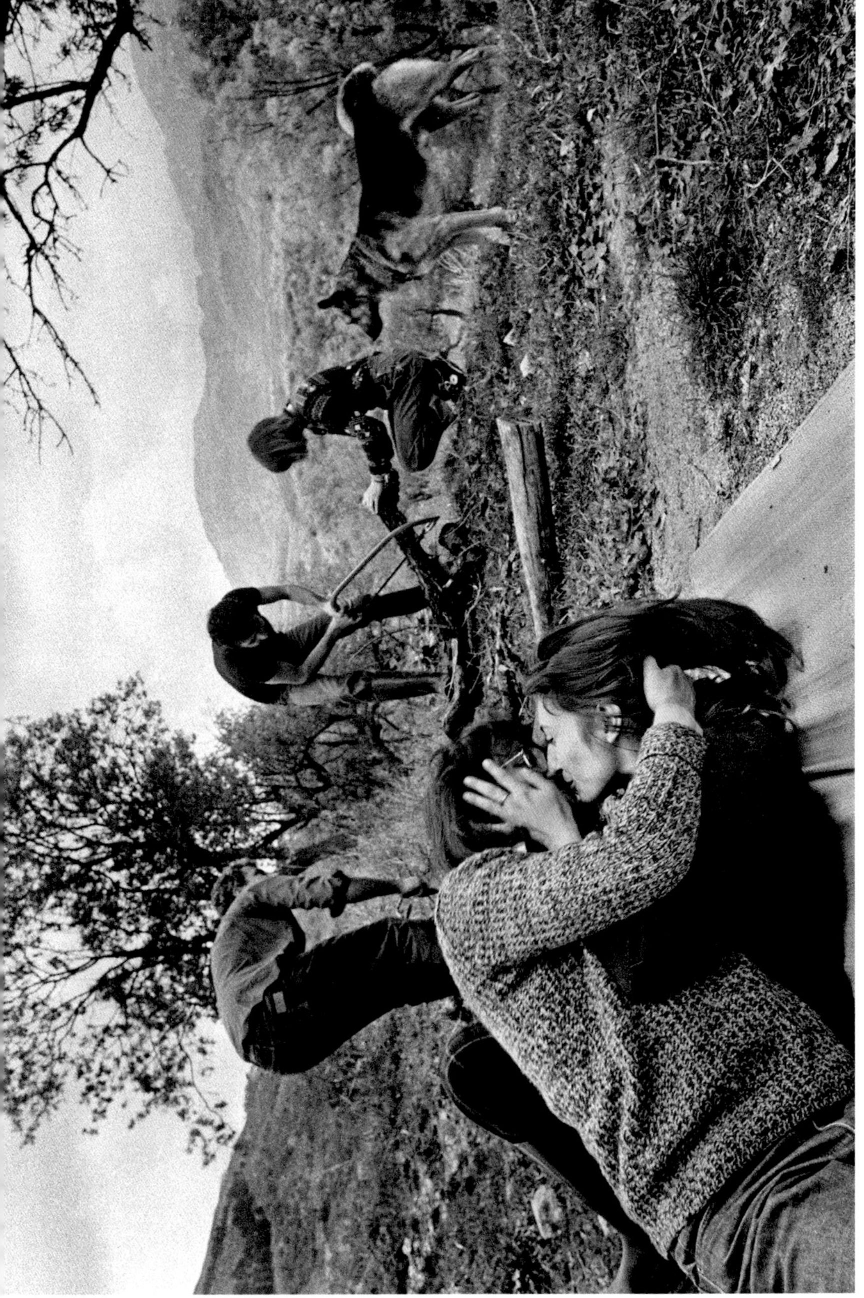

6. *Albergheria neighbourhood*, Palermo, 1977.

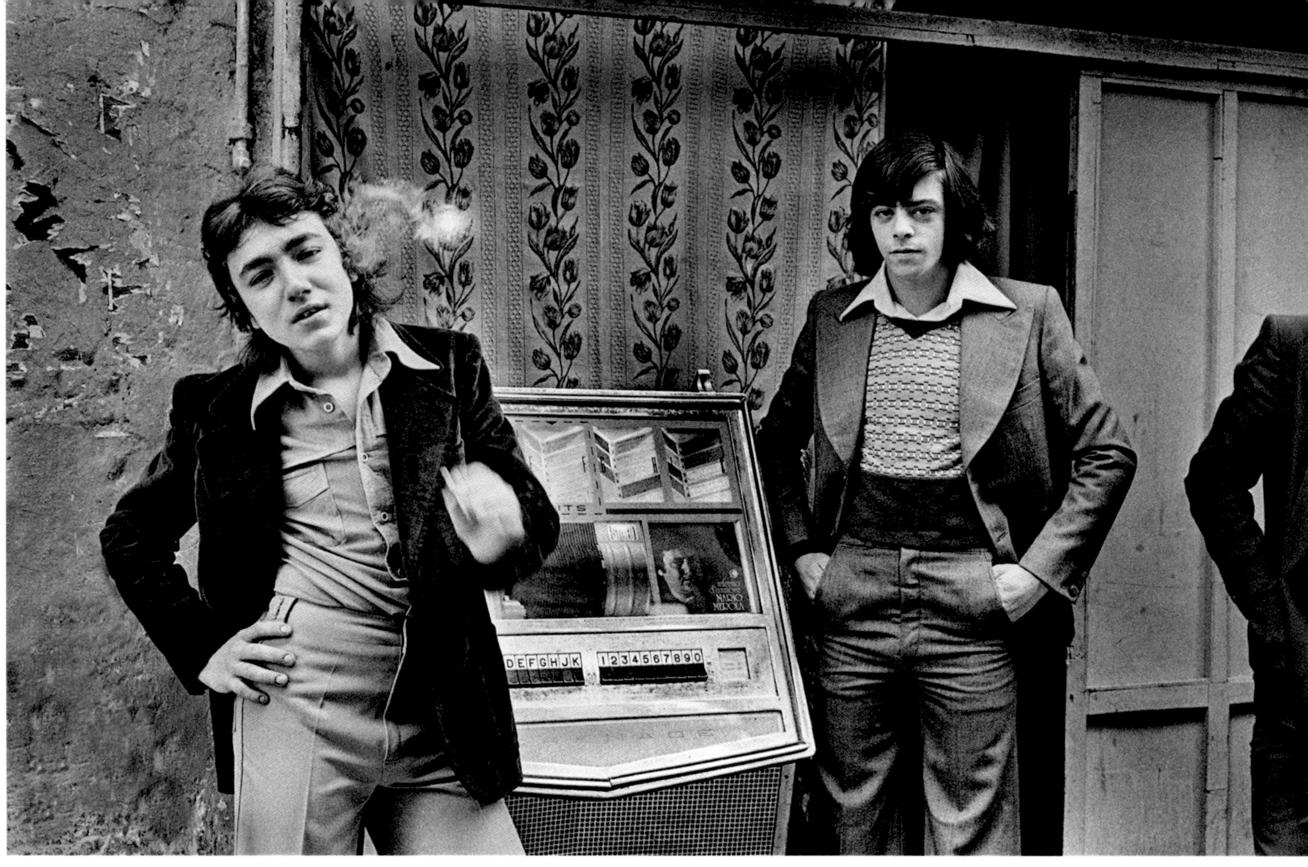
DEFGHJK
1234567890

7. Casa Professa. The rich bride stumbles over her veil, Palermo, 1980.

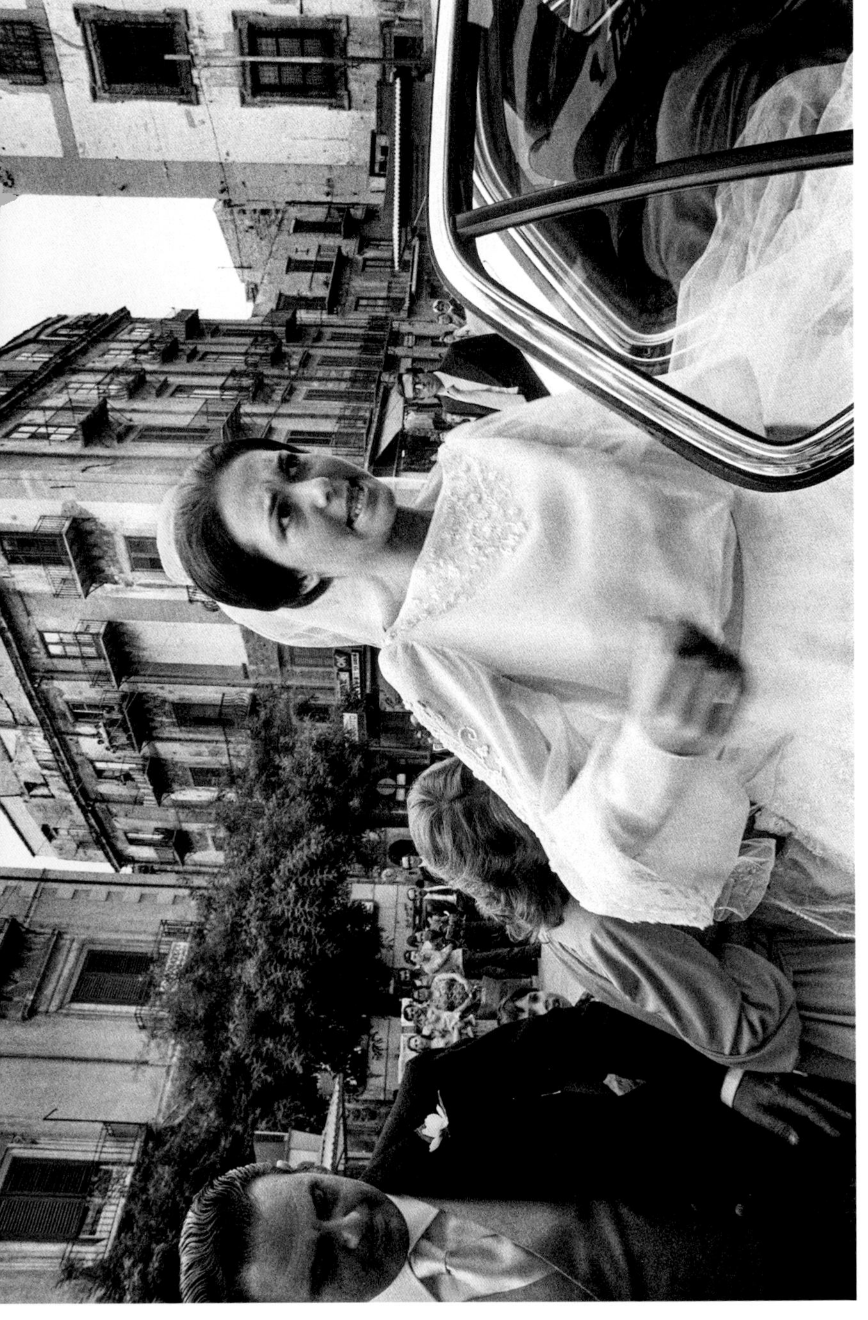

8. *Pier Paolo Pasolini at Circolo Turati*, Milan, 1972.

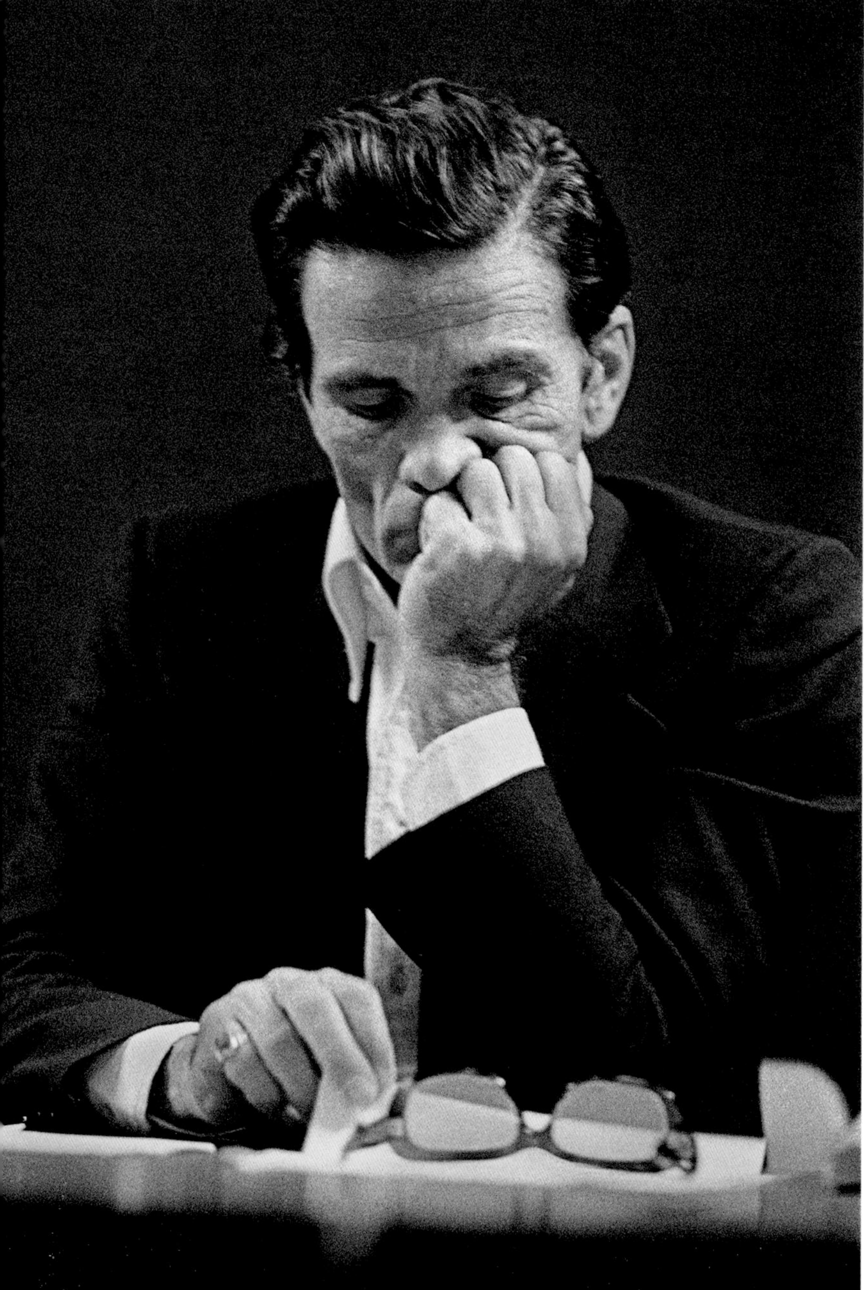

9. *Dario Fo at the Palazzina Liberty*, Milan, 1974.

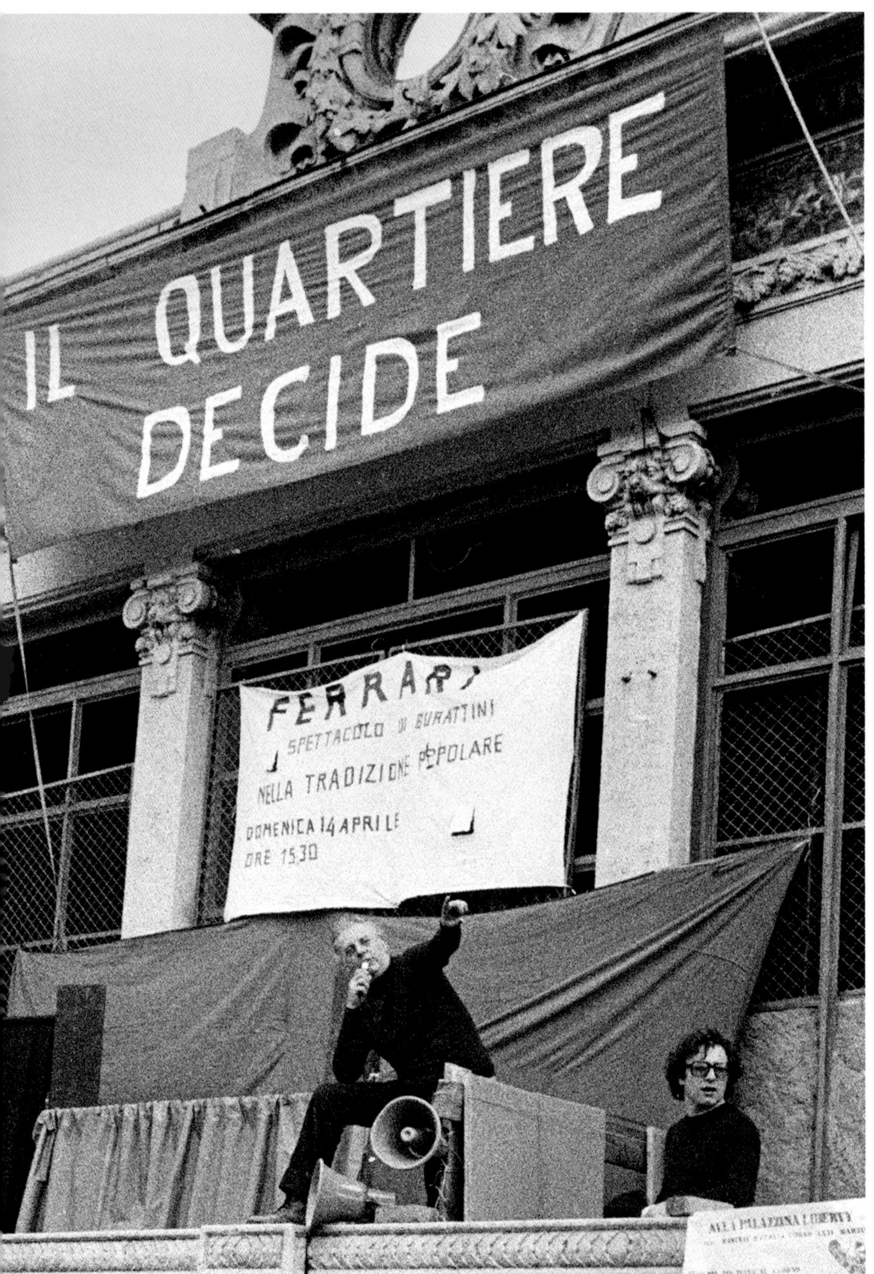

IL QUARTIERE
DECIDE
FERRARI
SPETTACOLO DI BURATTINI
NELLA TRADIZIONE POPOLARE
DOMENICA 14 APRILE
ORE 15.30

10. *Franca Rame at the Palazzina Liberty*, Milan, 1974.

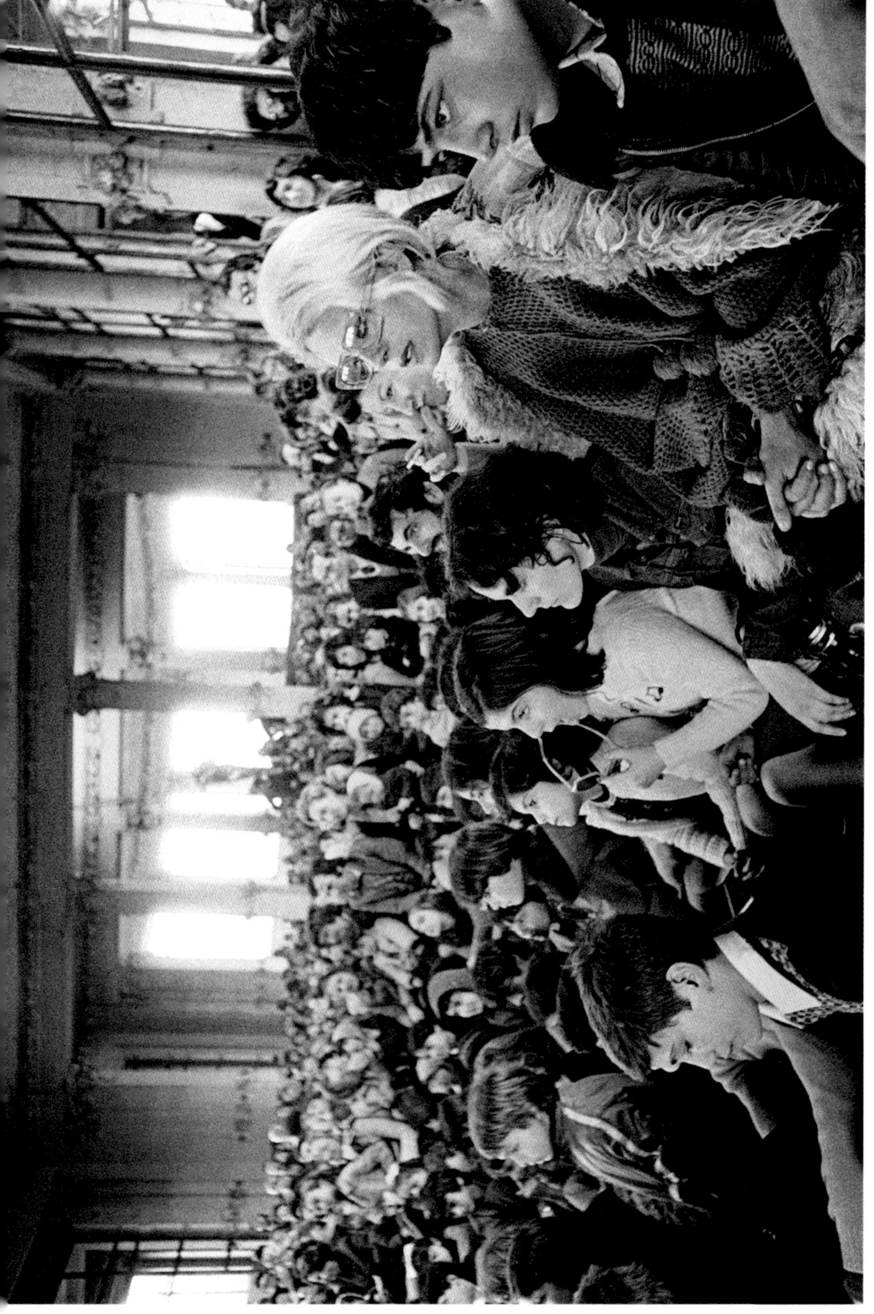

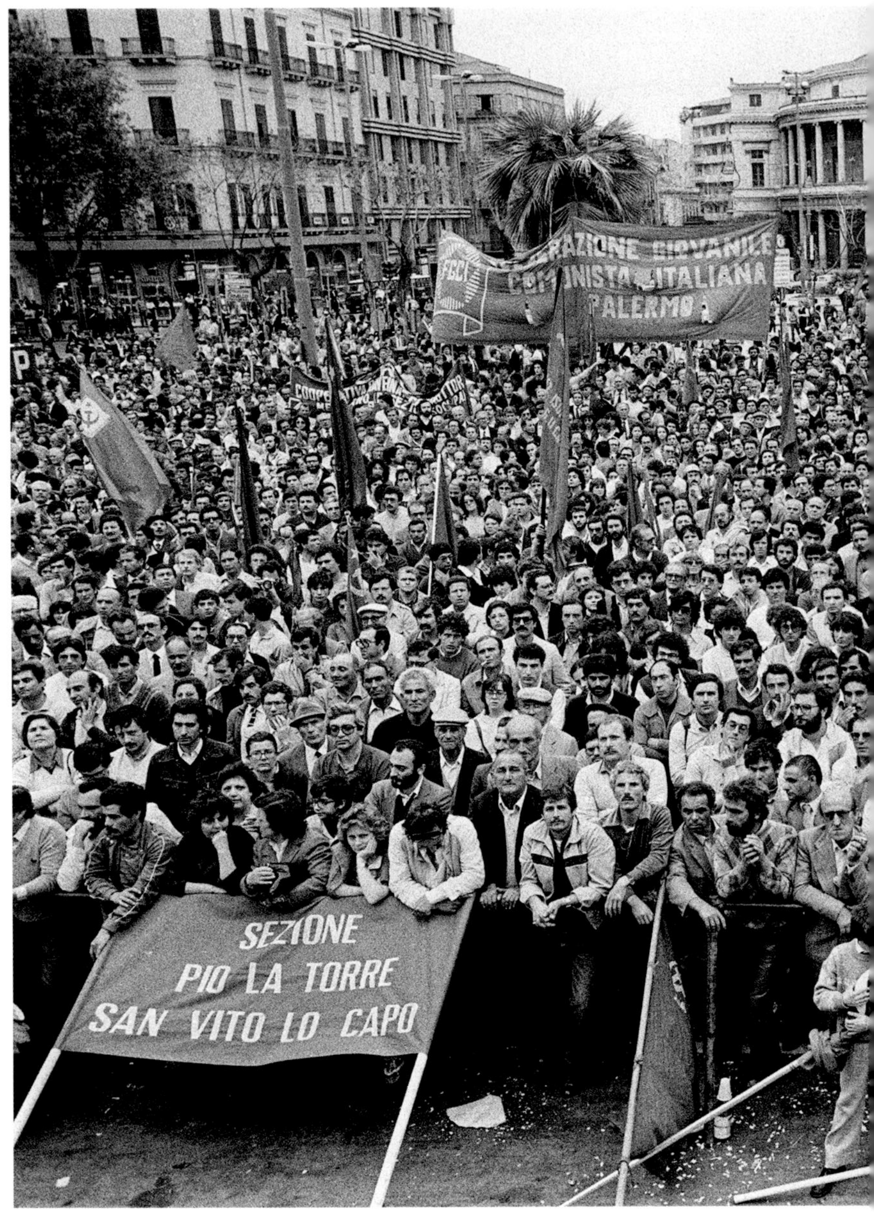

11. *PCI rally in Piazza Politeama*, Palermo, 1983.

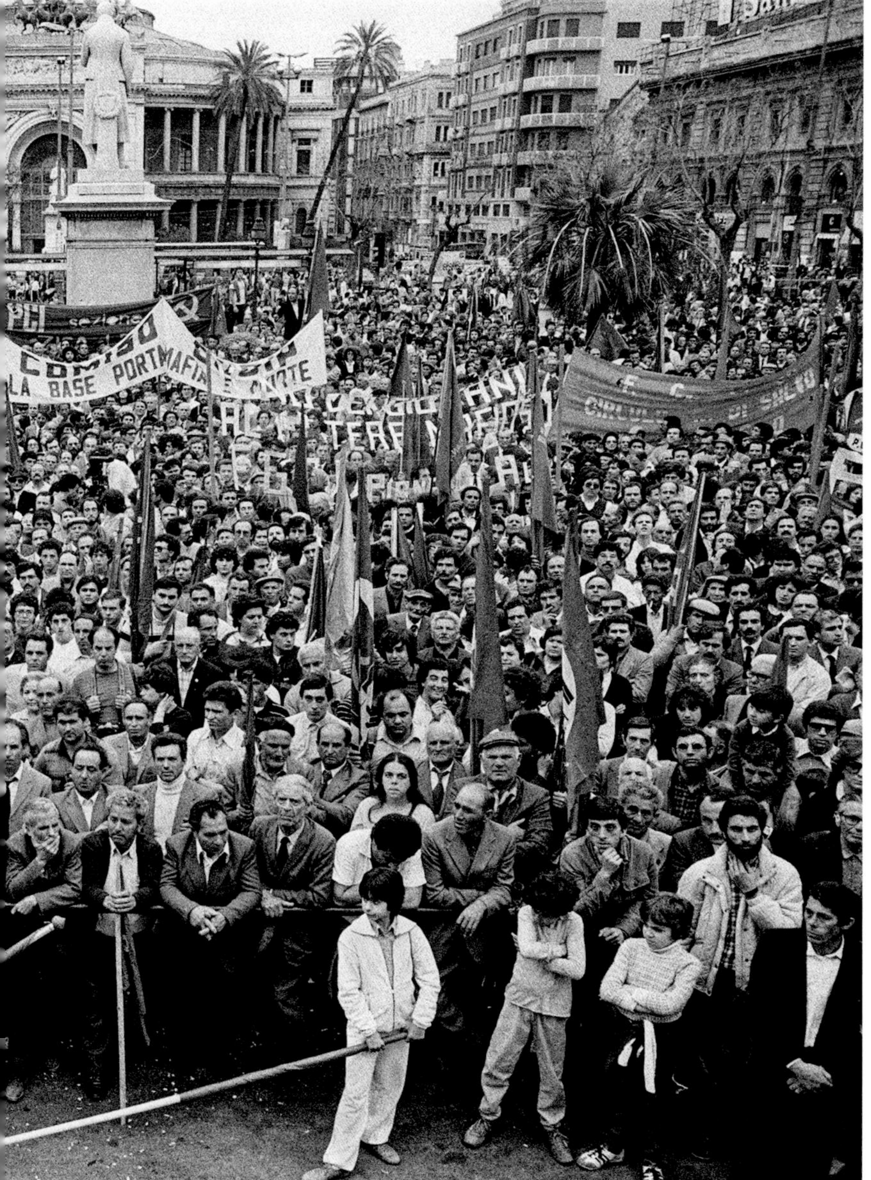

12. *A cat and a rat satiated with rubbish*, Palermo, 1977

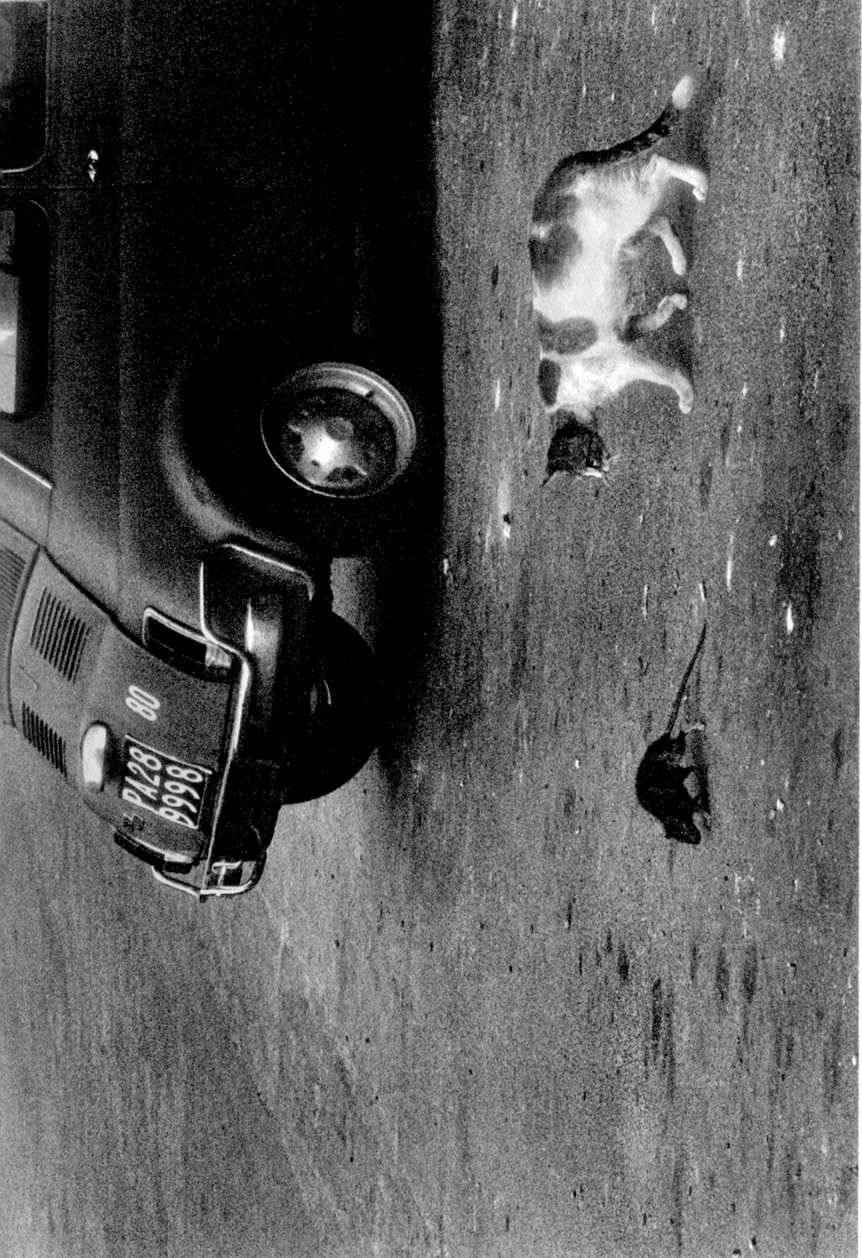

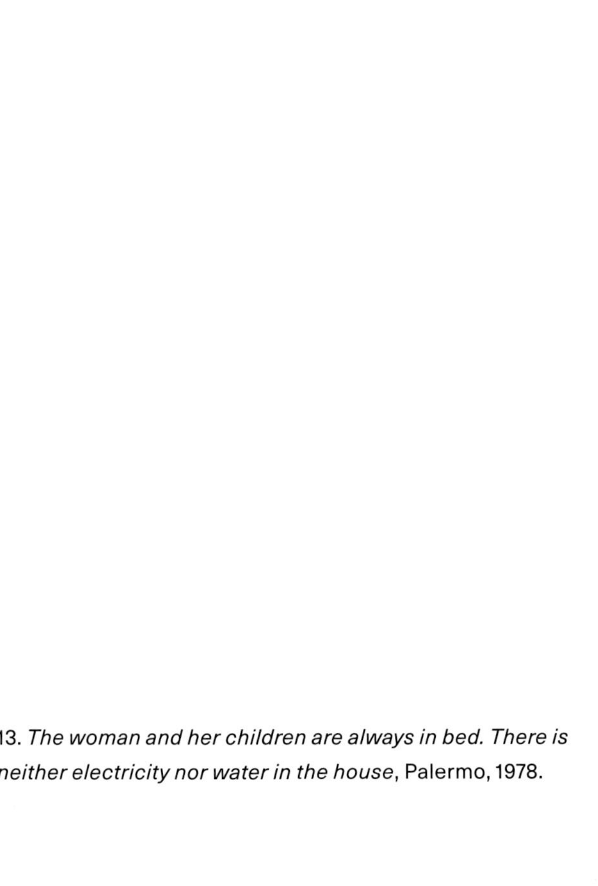

13. *The woman and her children are always in bed. There is neither electricity nor water in the house*, Palermo, 1978.

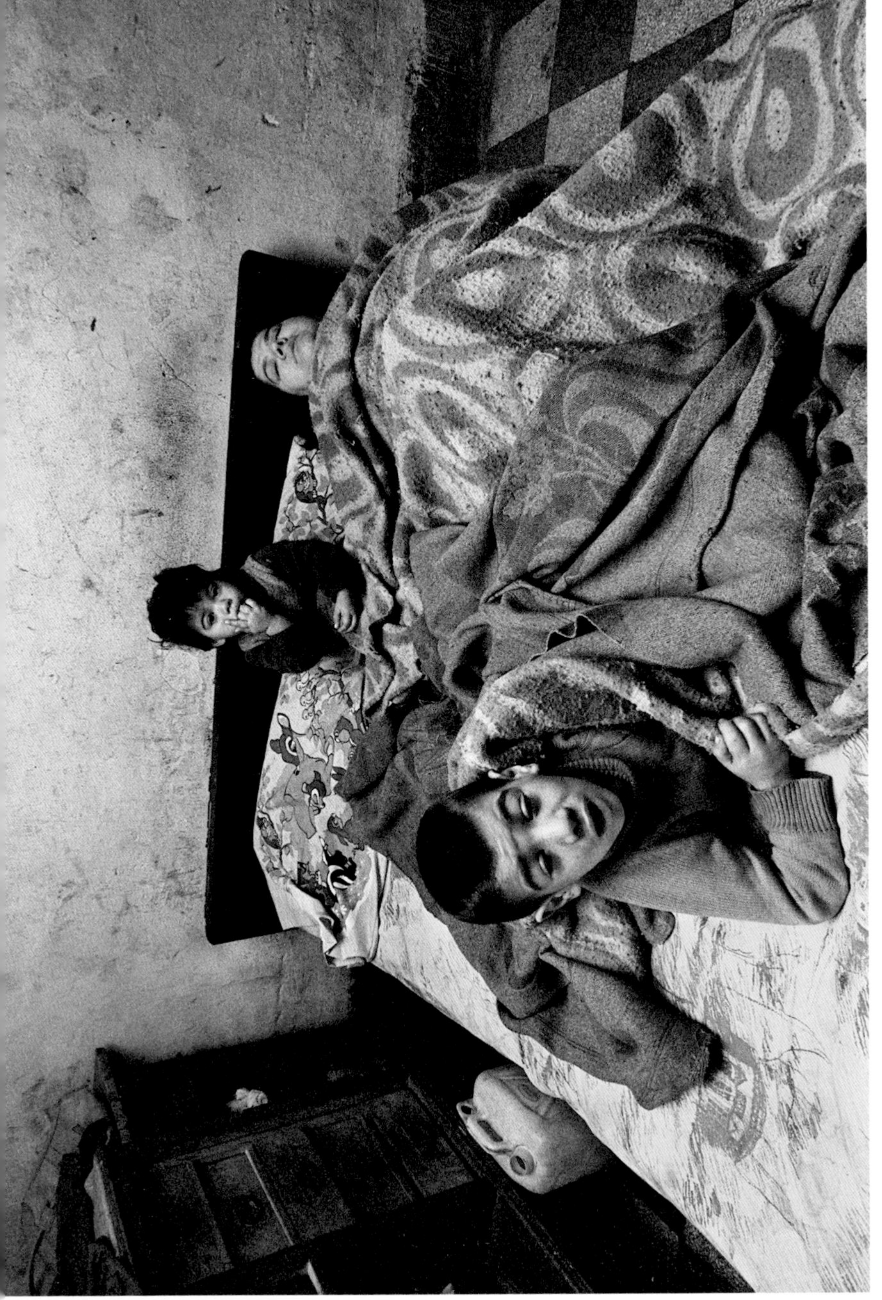

14. *At night, the infant cried desperately. His mother, too tired, had not woken up while a rat was gnawing a finger off his left hand*, Palermo, 1978.

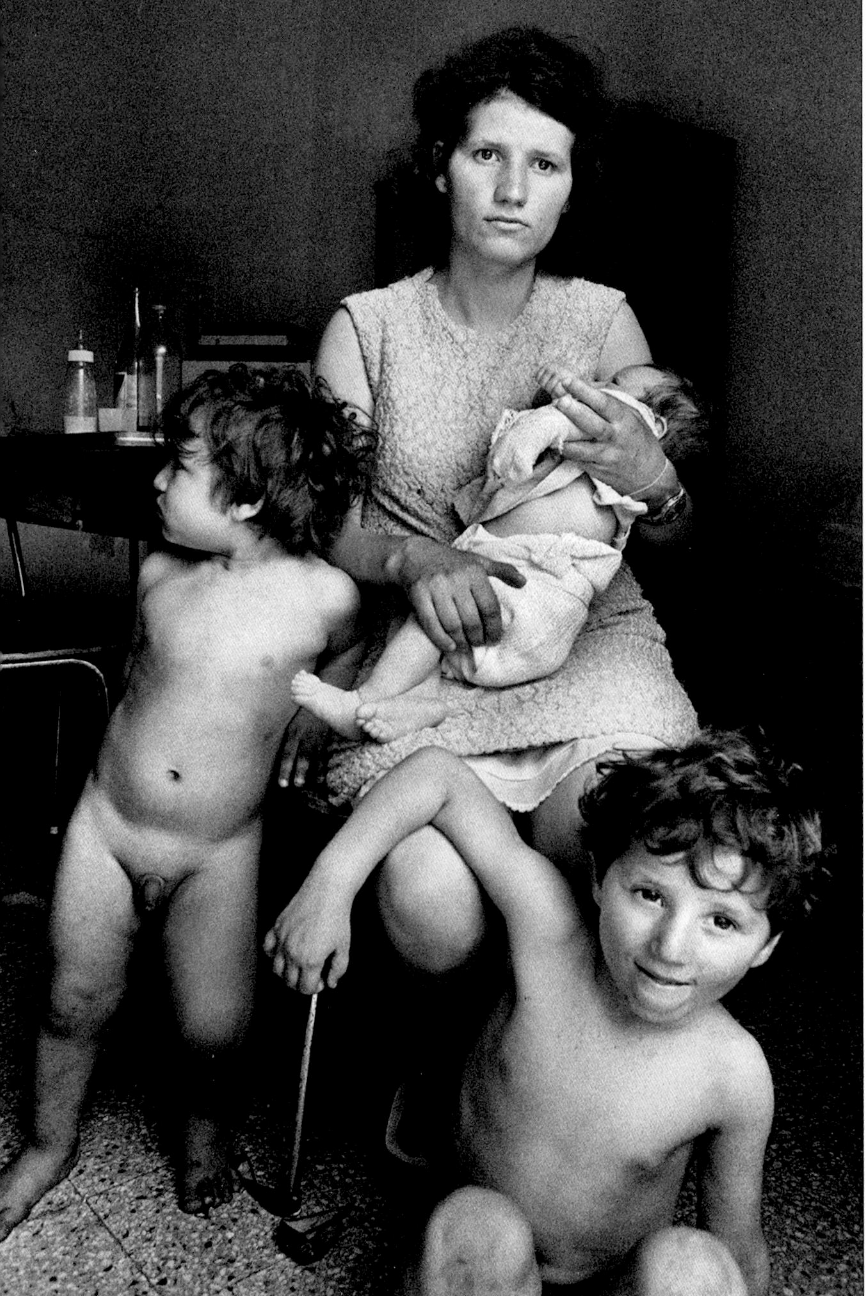

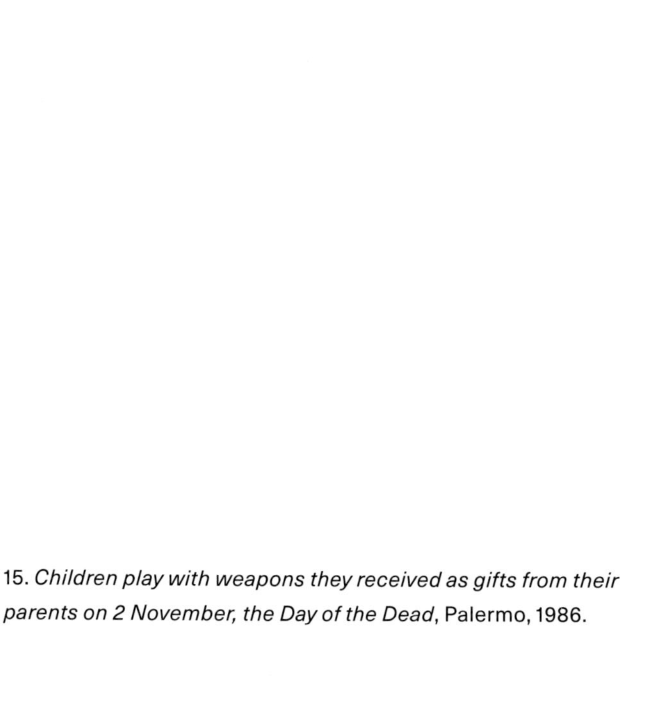

15. *Children play with weapons they received as gifts from their parents on 2 November, the Day of the Dead*, Palermo, 1986.

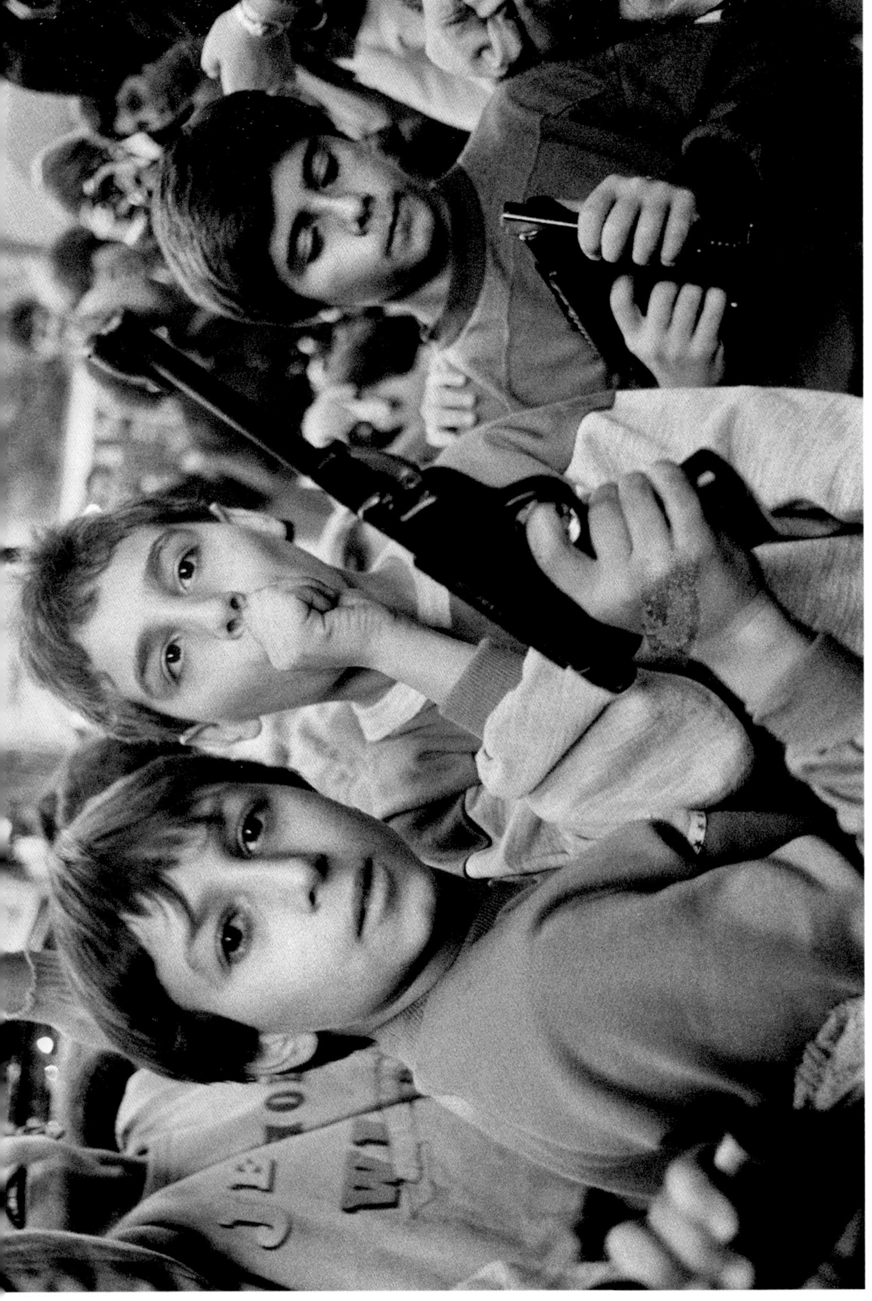

16. *Near the church of Santa Chiara. The killer's game*, Palermo, 1982.

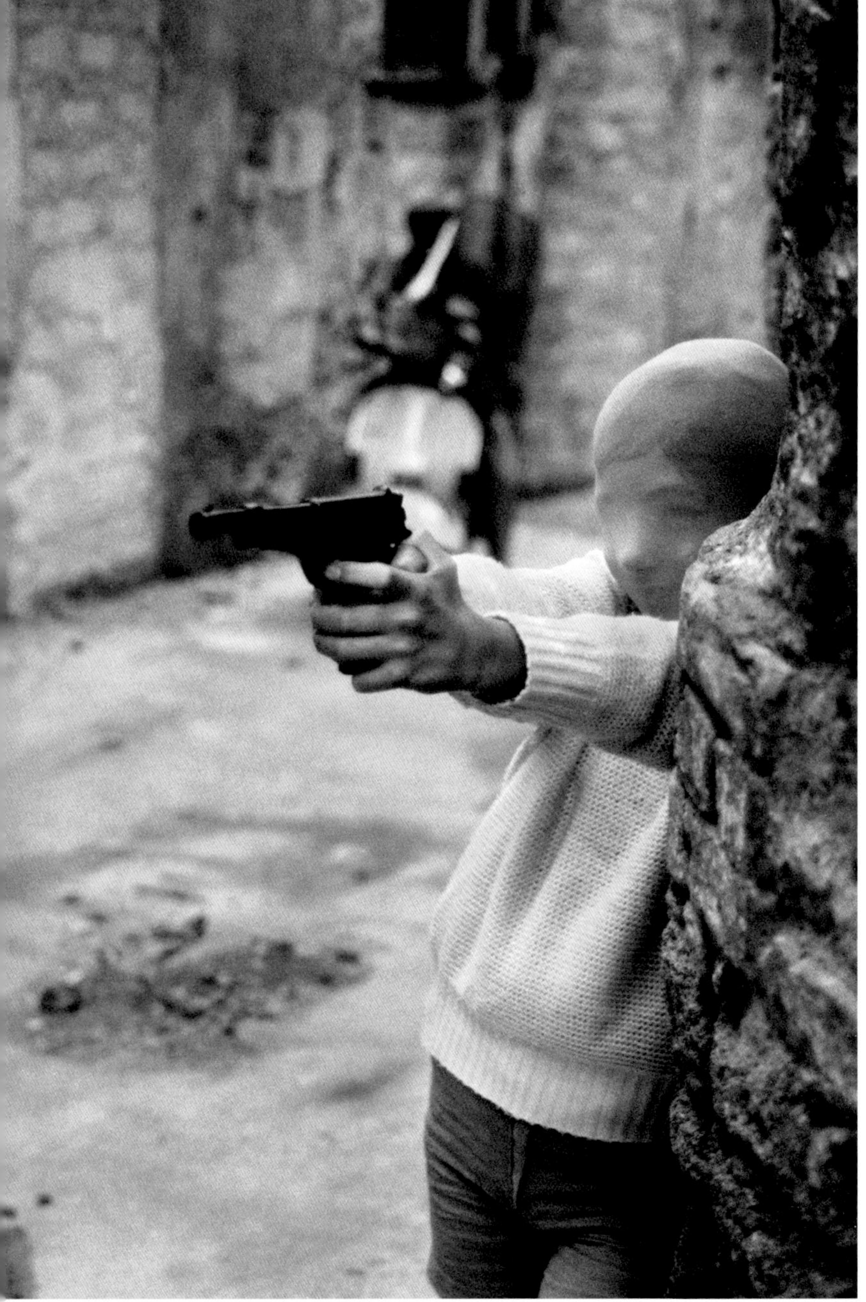

17. *The family watches over the late father in the entrance to the poor home*, Palermo, 1986.

Overleaf:
18. *Family at the funeral of their son who died in hospital*, San Vito Lo Capo, 1980.

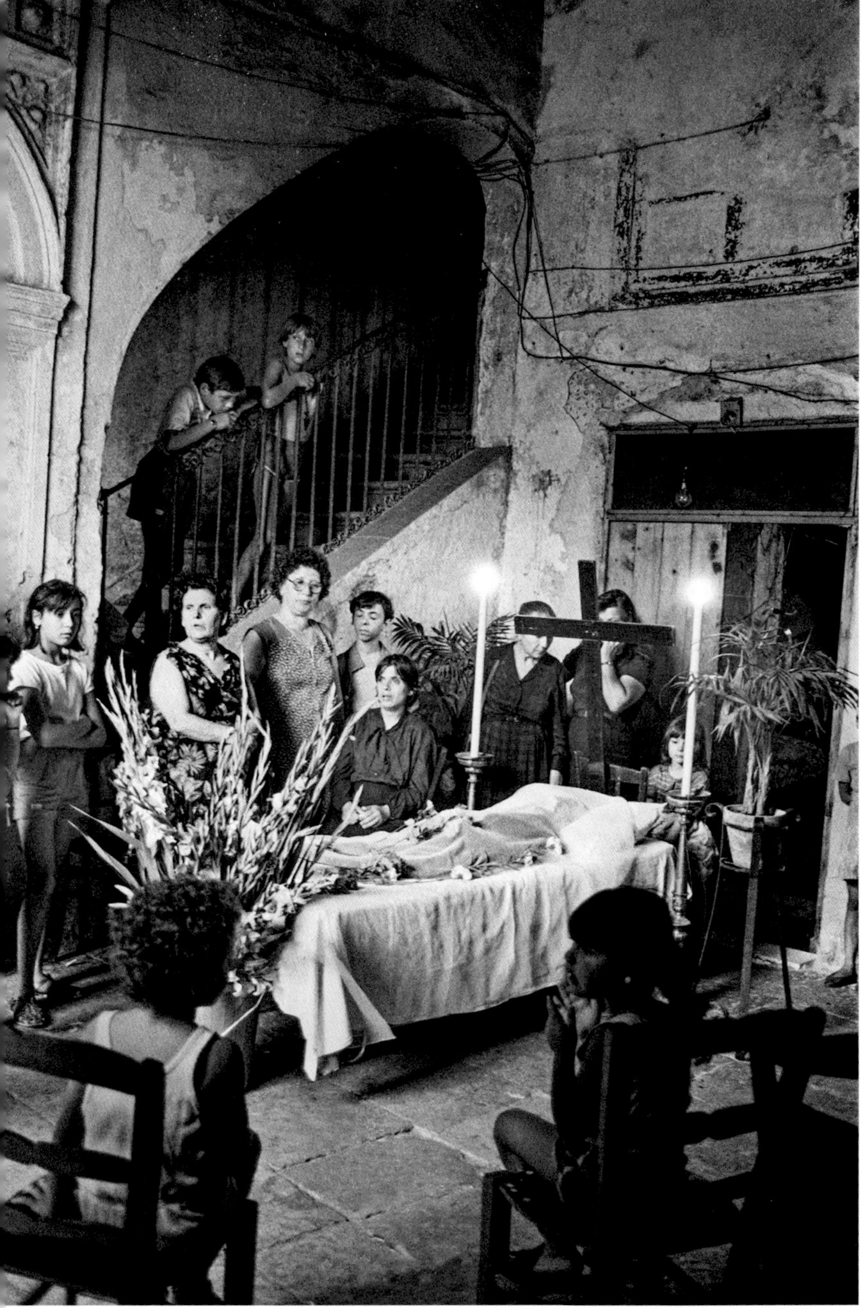

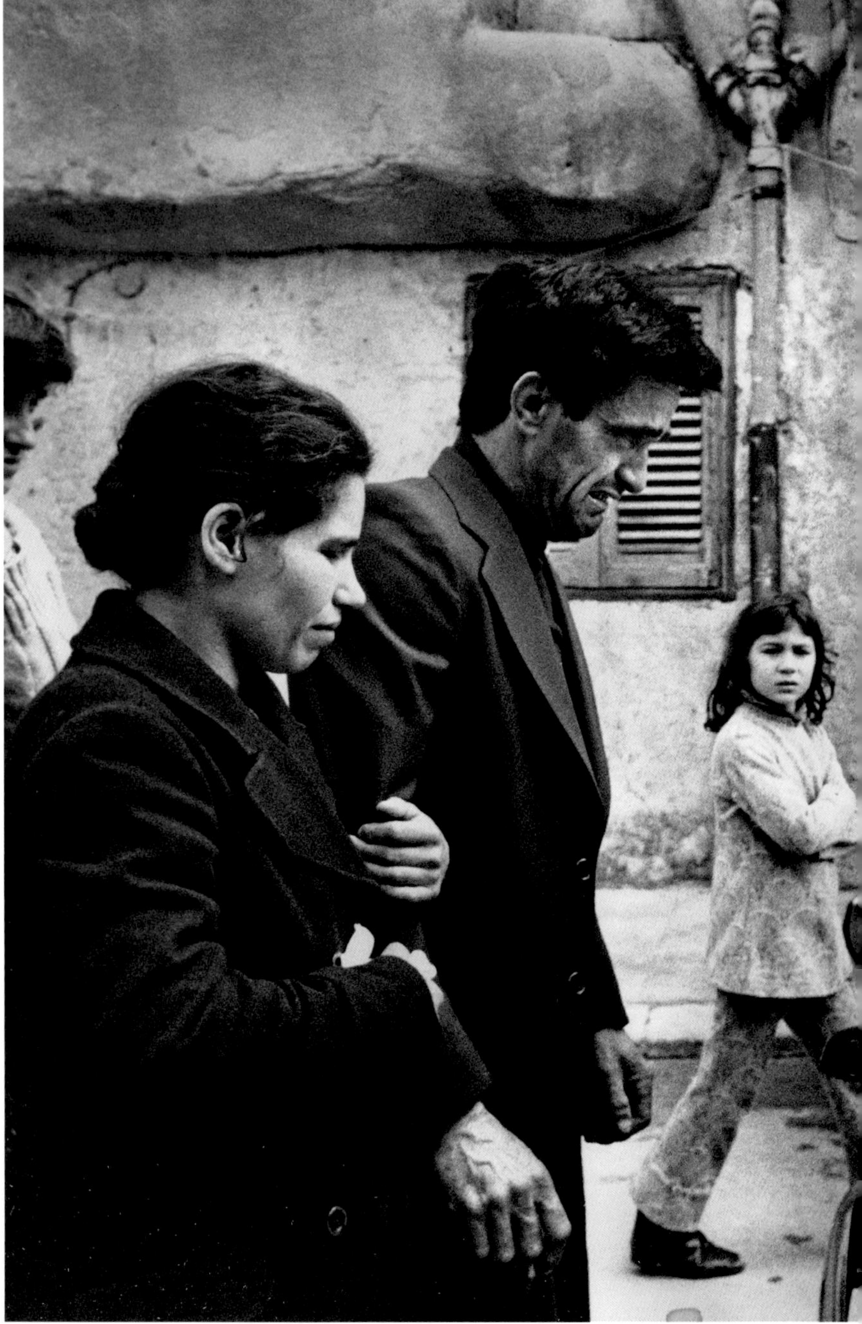

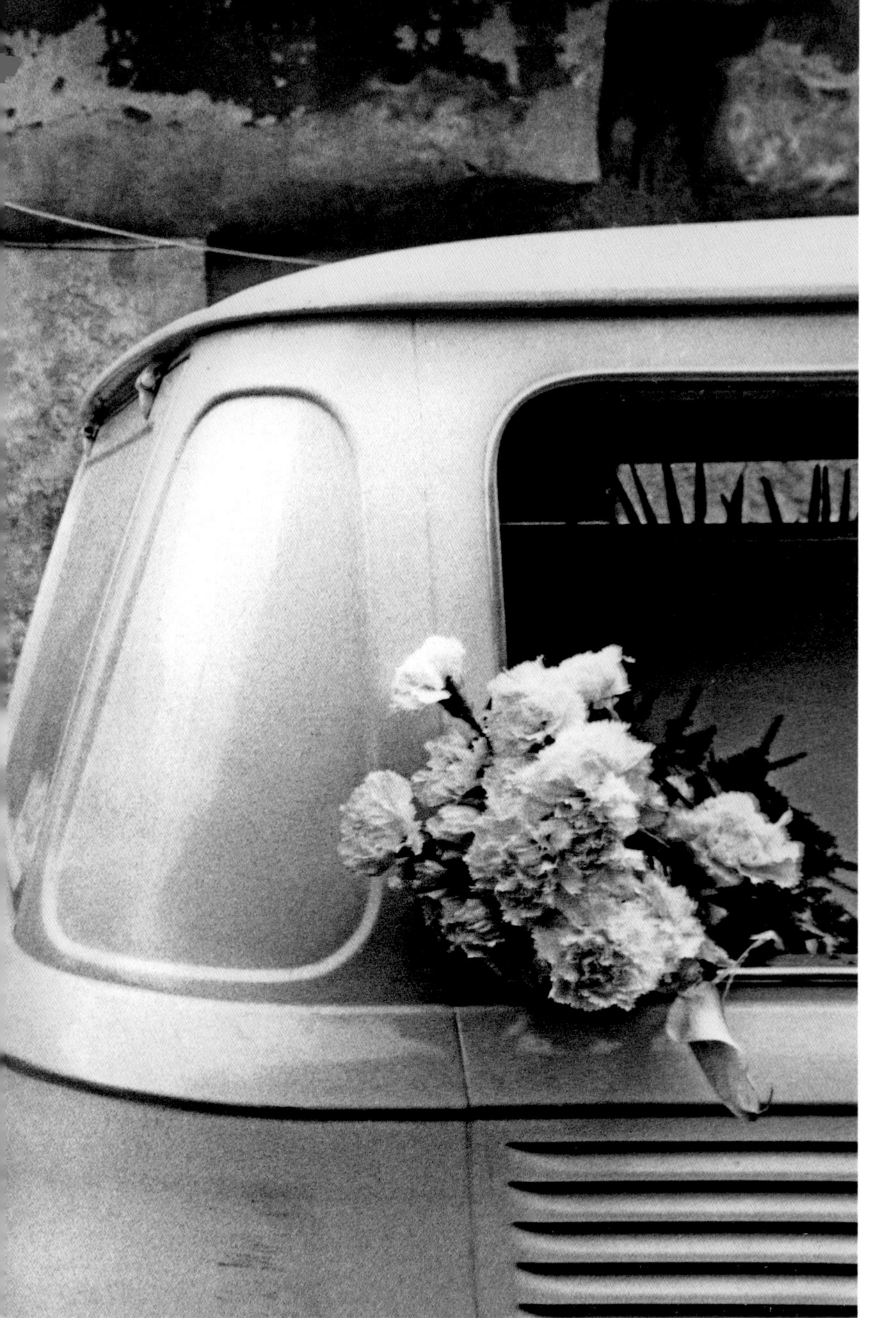

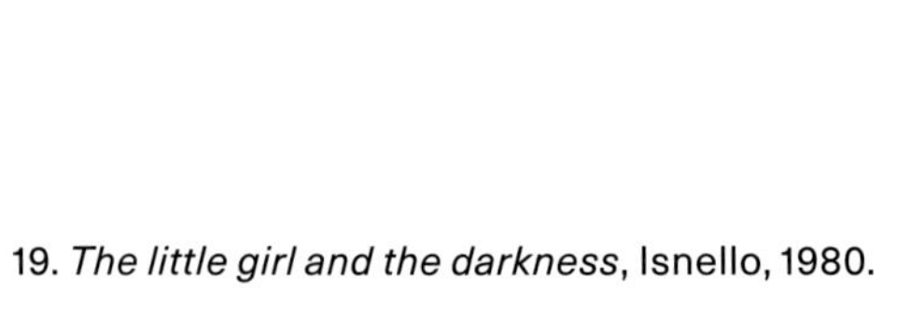

19. *The little girl and the darkness*, Isnello, 1980.

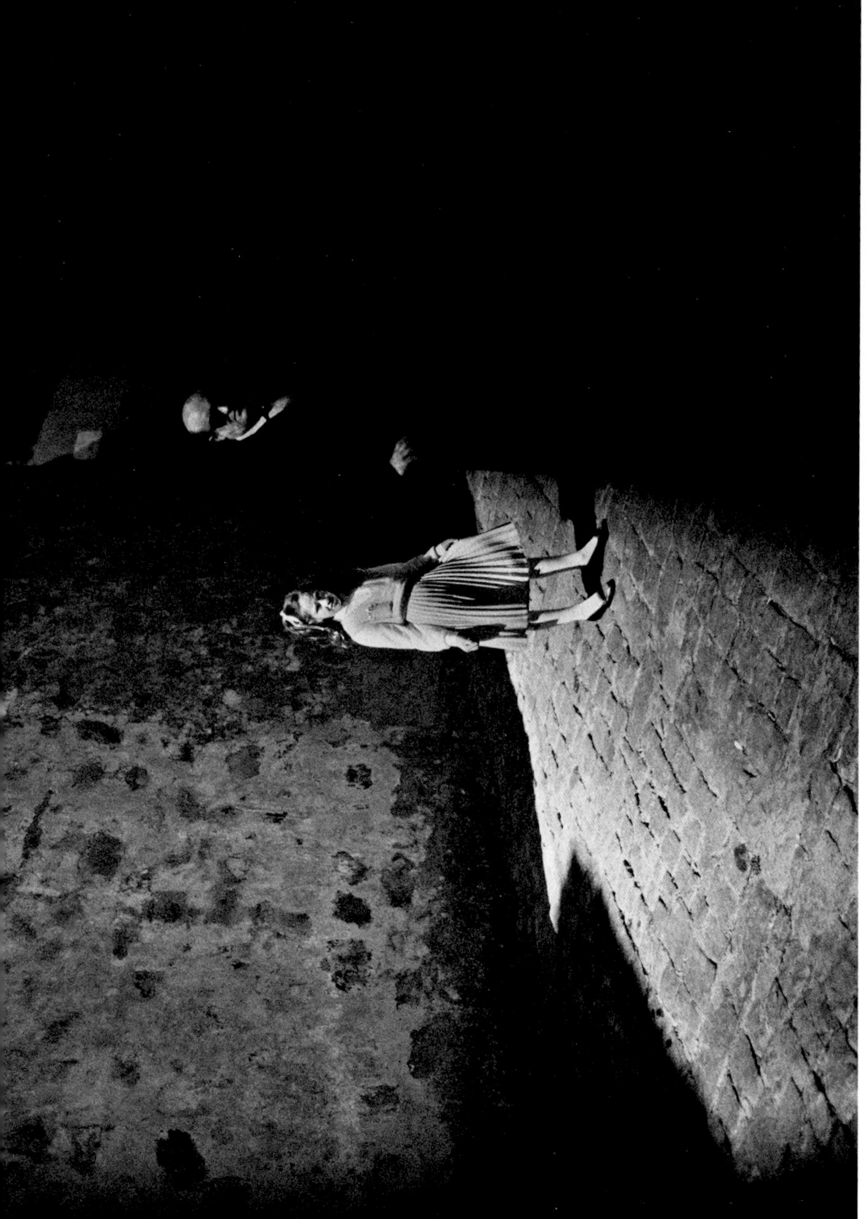

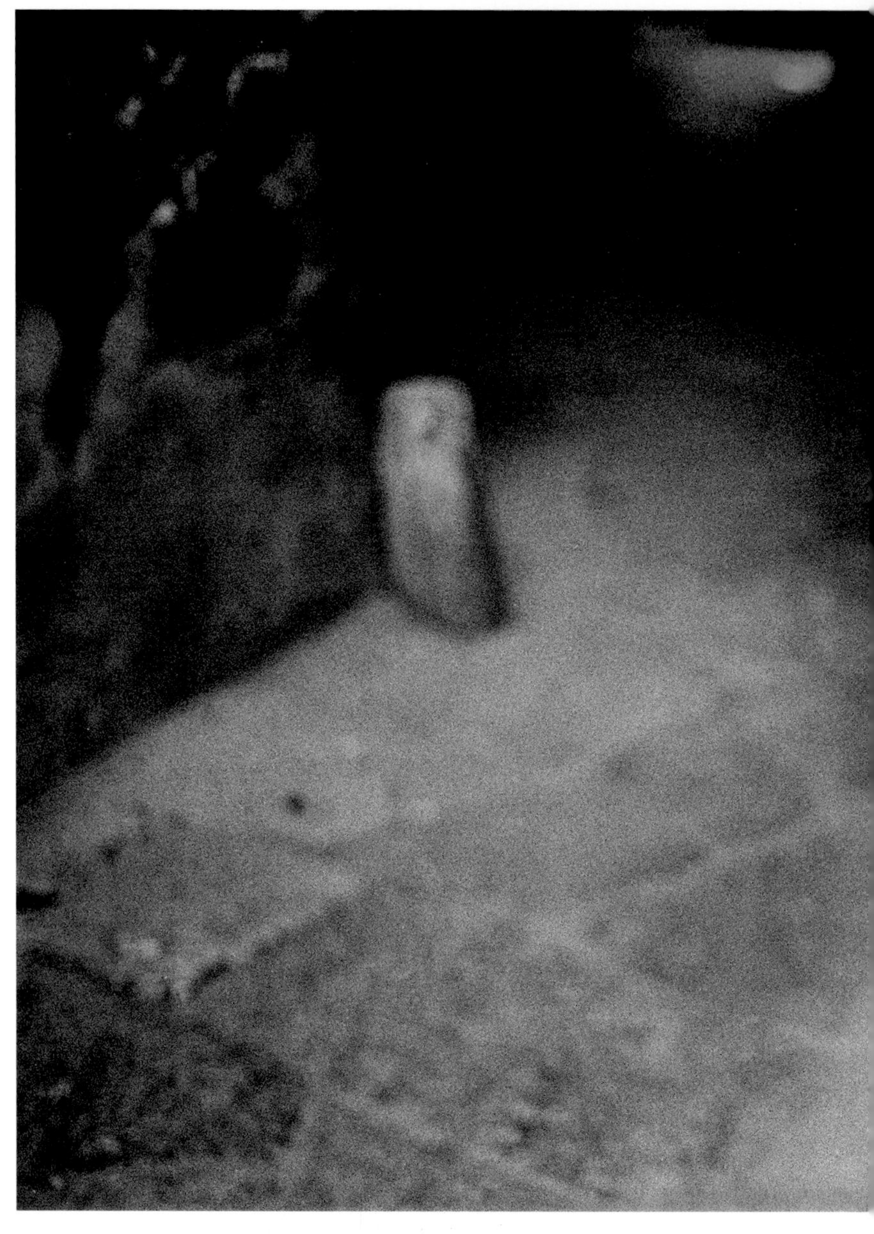

20. *Via Calderai*, Palermo, 1991.

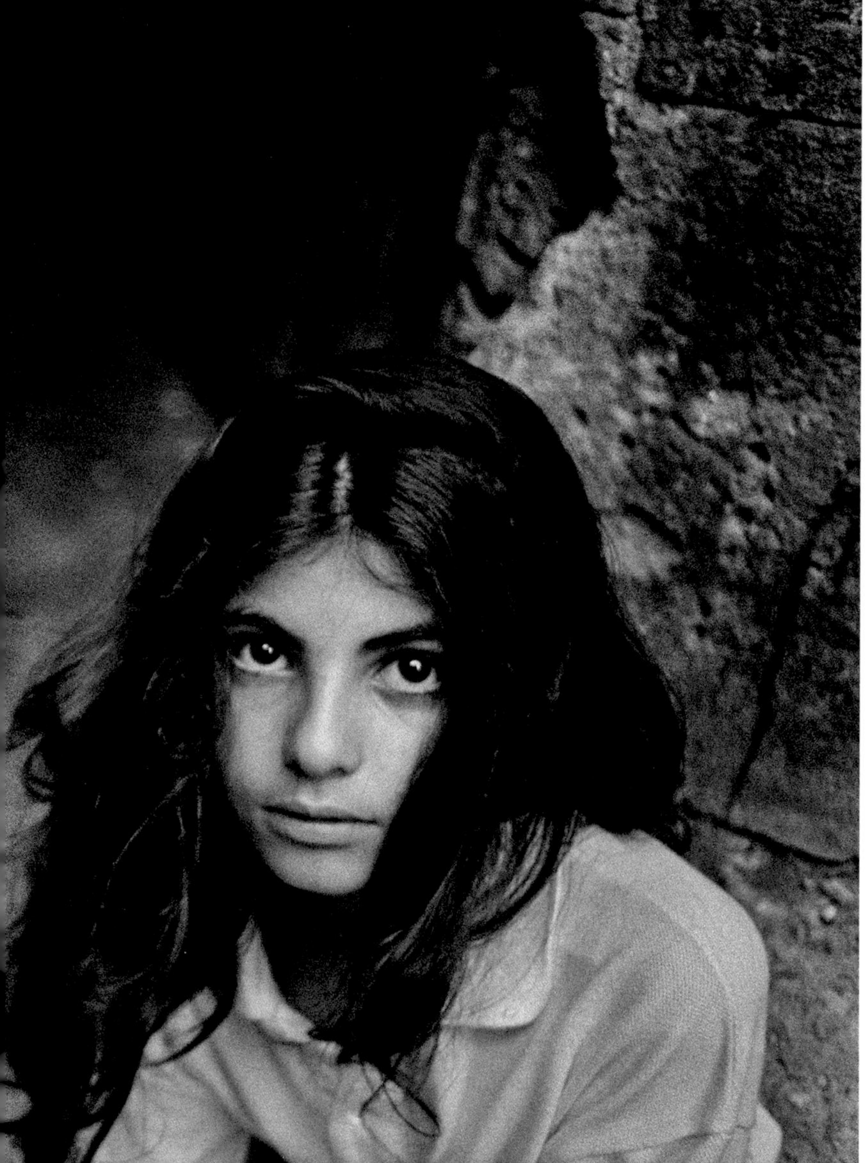

21. *The dishwasher girl*, Monreale, 1979.

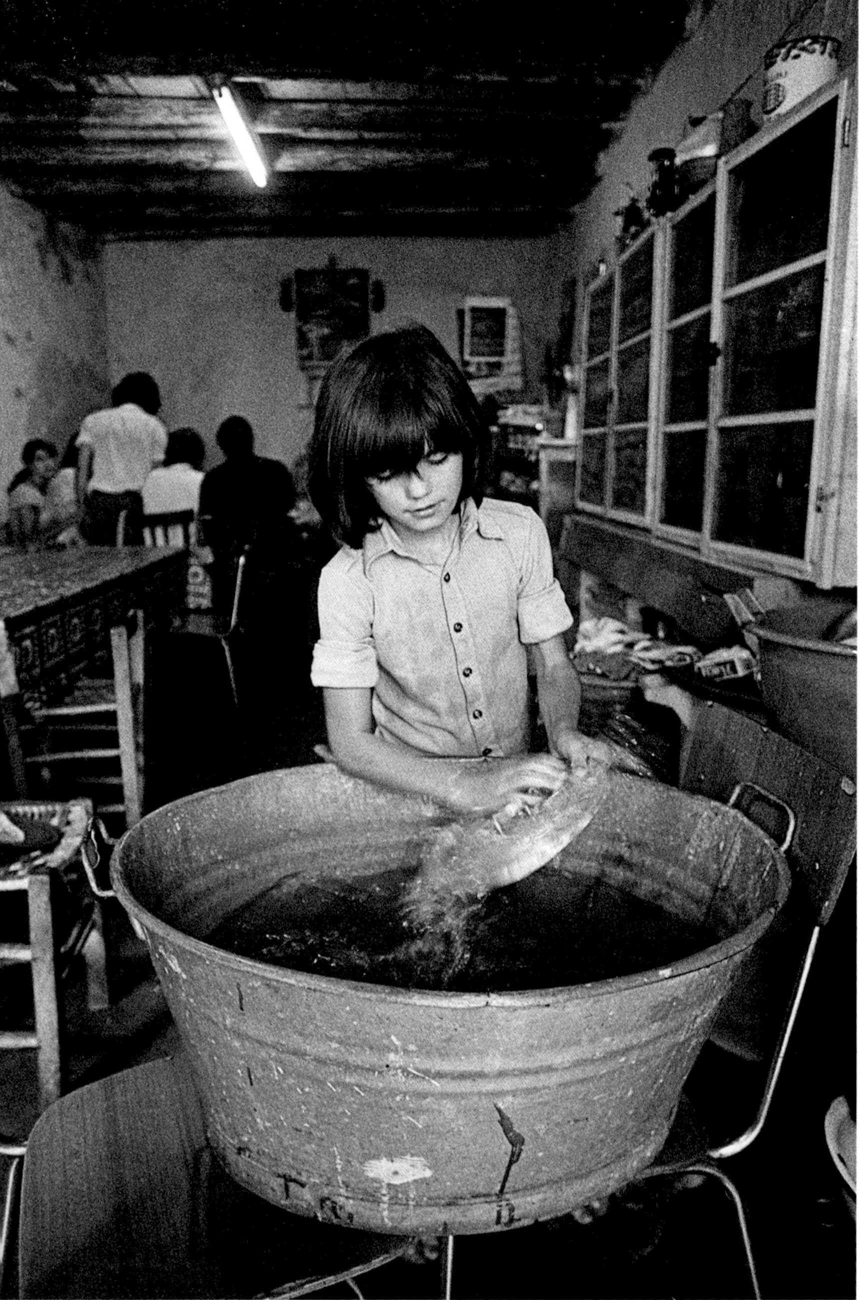

22. *The embroiderer*, Montemaggiore Belsito, 1987.

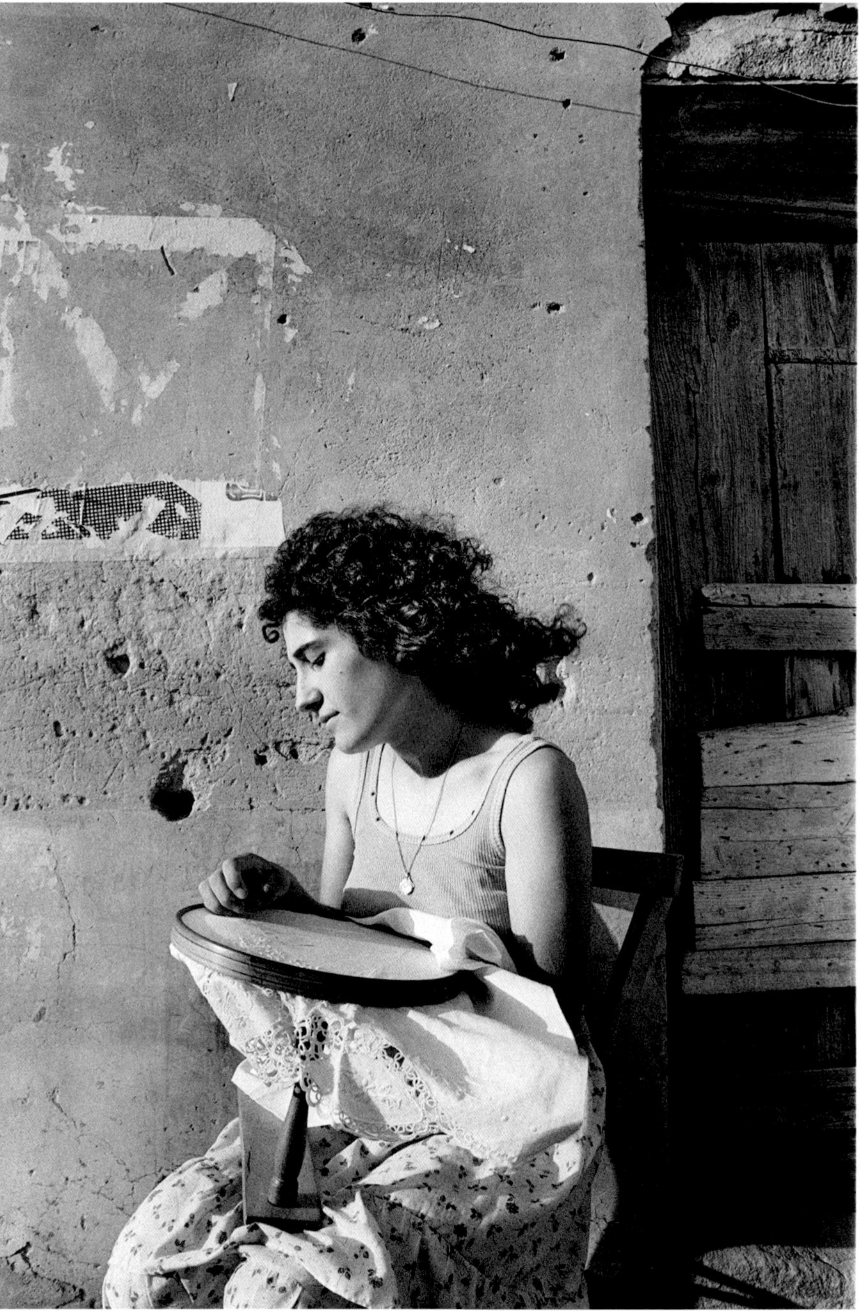

23. *Aristocratic garden reception with dead fox*, Palermo, 1987.

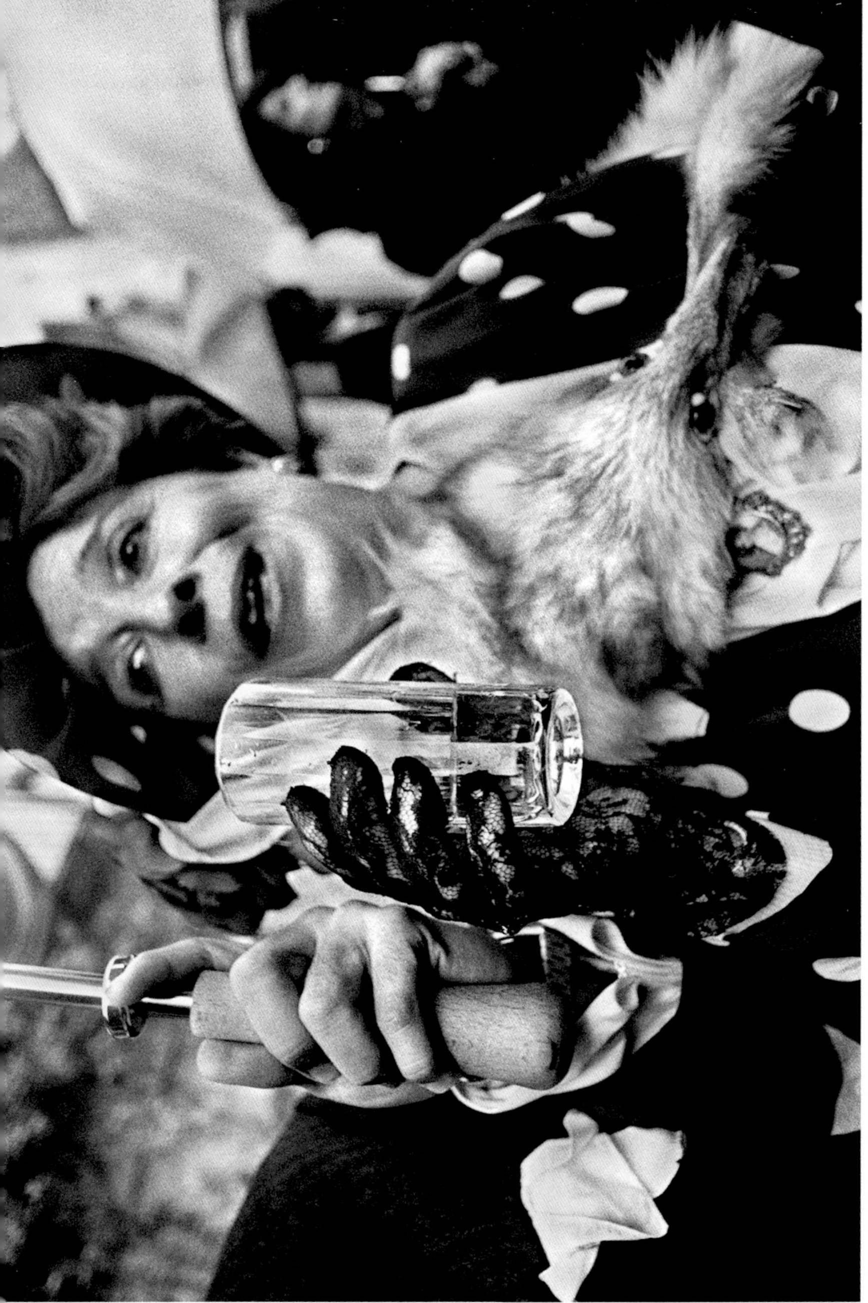

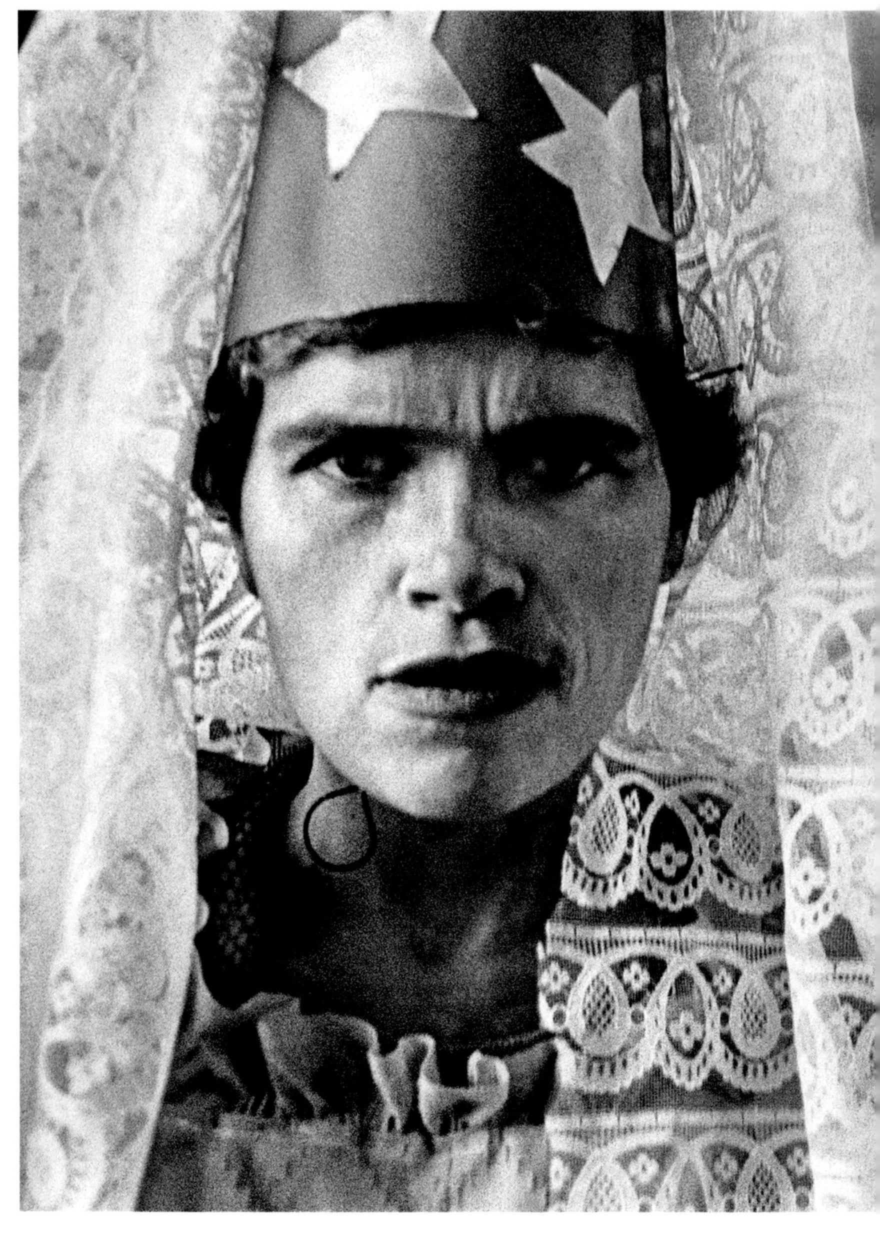

24. *Via Pindemonte. Carnival party at the psychiatric hospital*, Palermo, 1986.

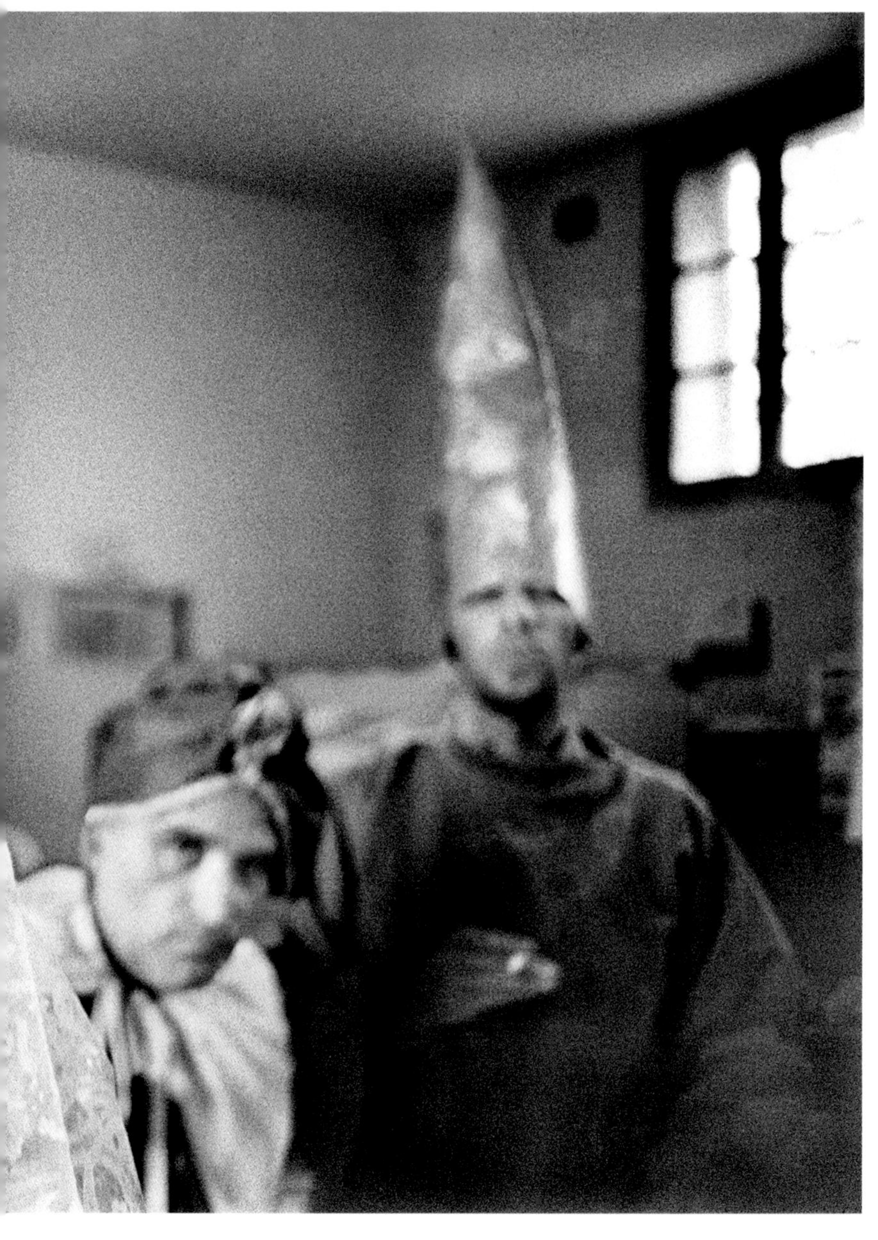

25. *New Year's Eve party at Villa Airoldi*, Palermo, 1985.

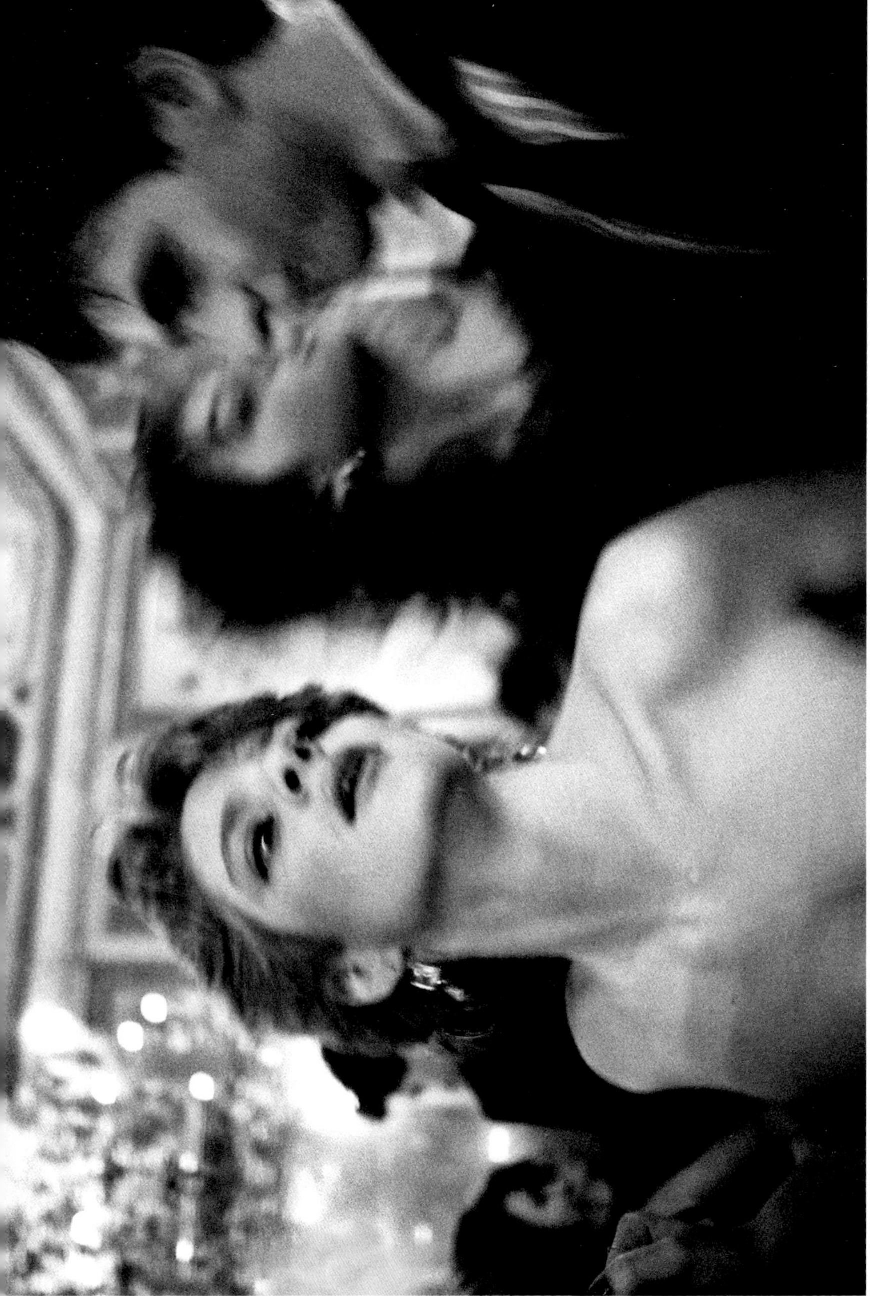

26. *Graziella. Via Pindemonte. Psychiatric hospital*, Palermo, 1983.

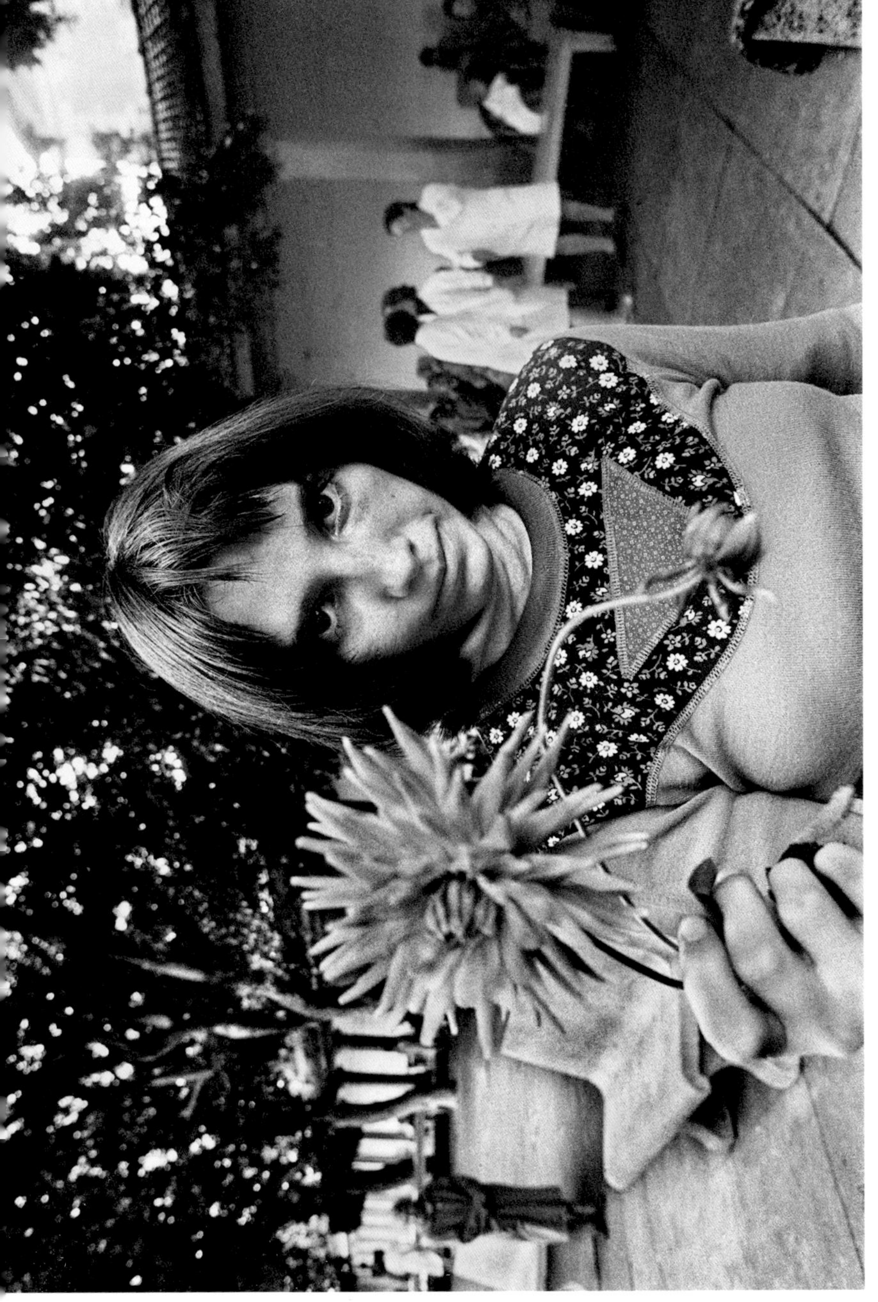

27. *Cala neighbourhood. The little girl with the ball*, Palermo, 1980.

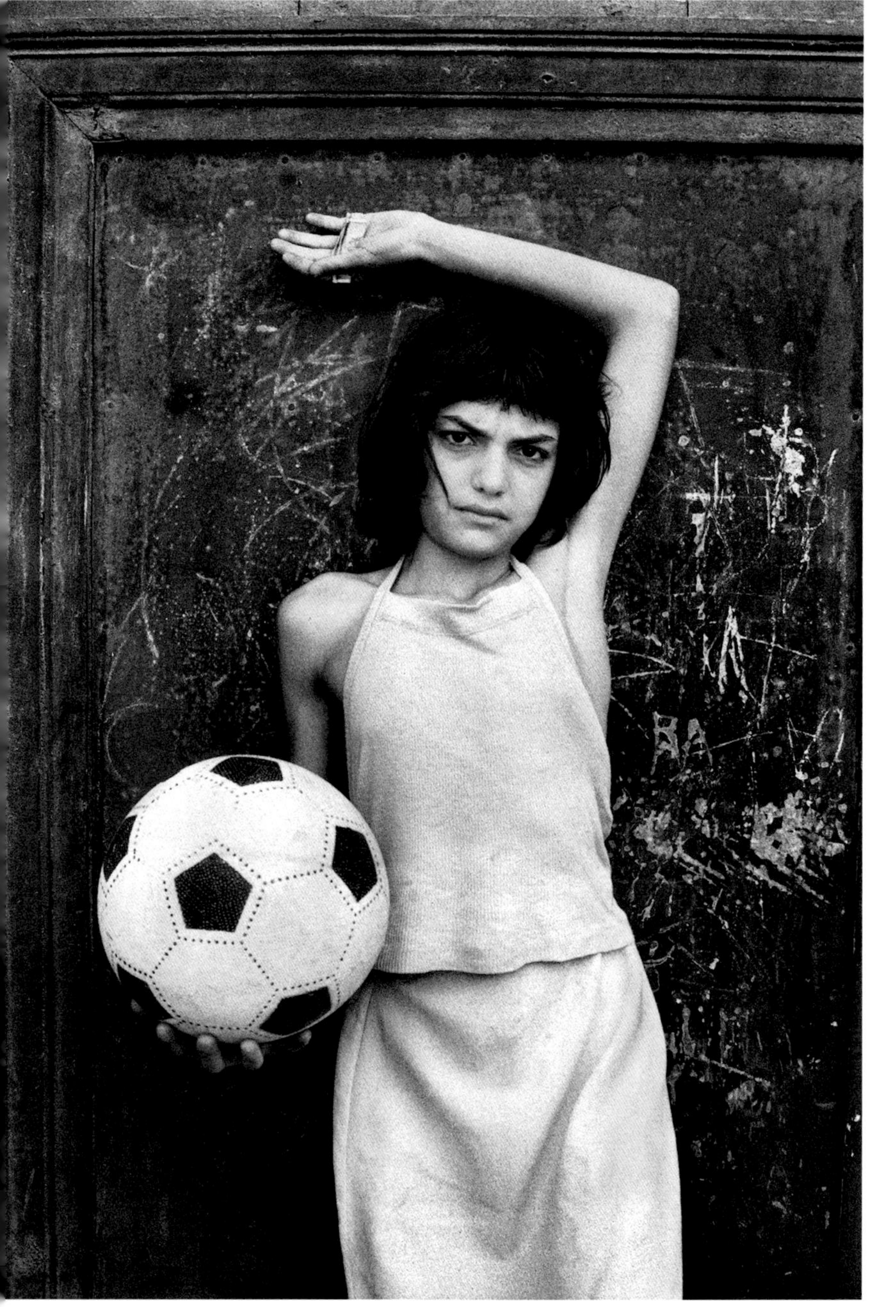

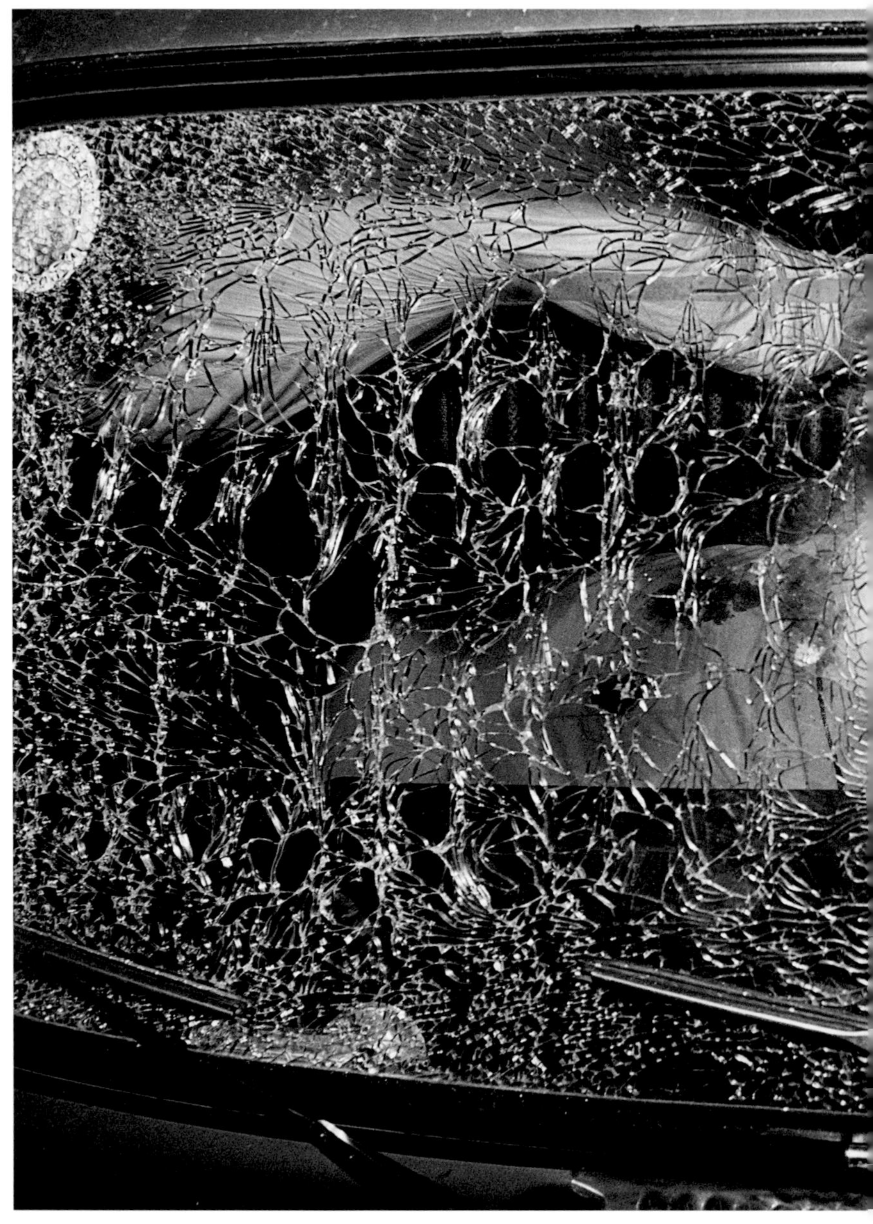

28. Palermo, 1977.

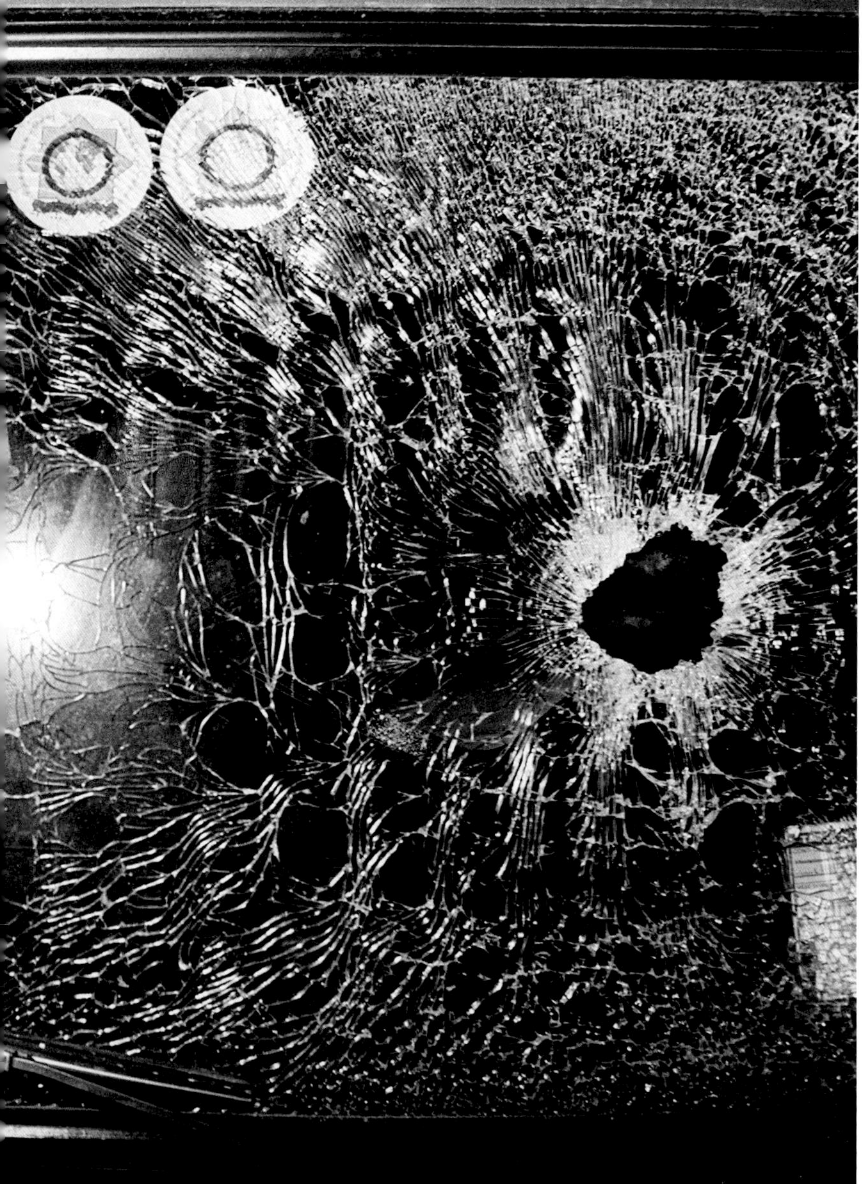

29. Trabia, 1975.

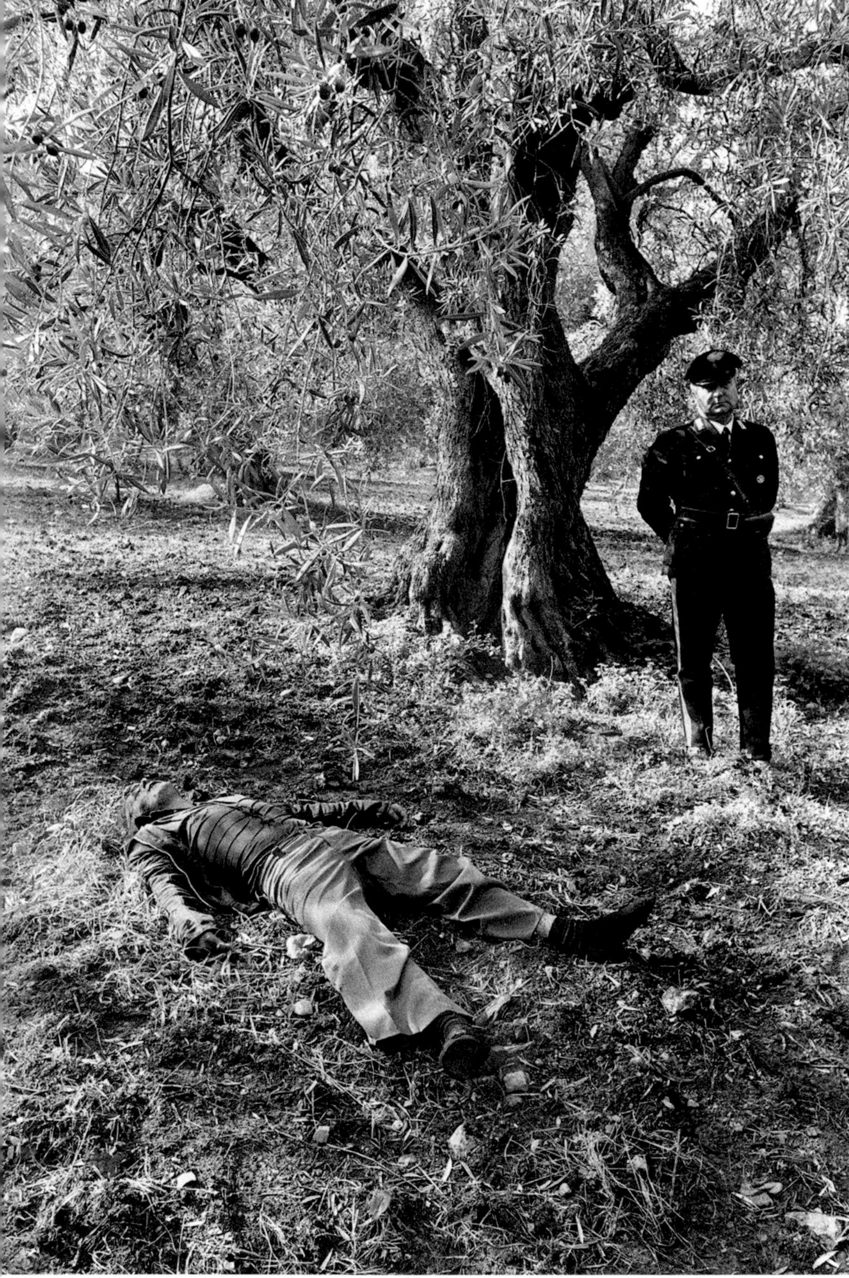

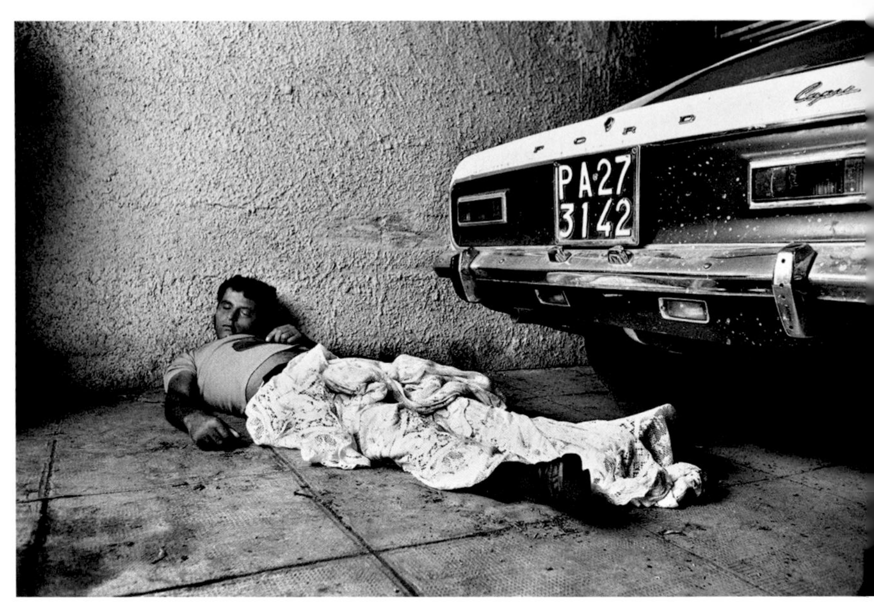

30. *Palermo murder*, 1975.

31. *Antonino Battaglia had gone out to buy cannoli, they killed him in the dark. His wife tried in vain to help him*, Palermo, 1976.

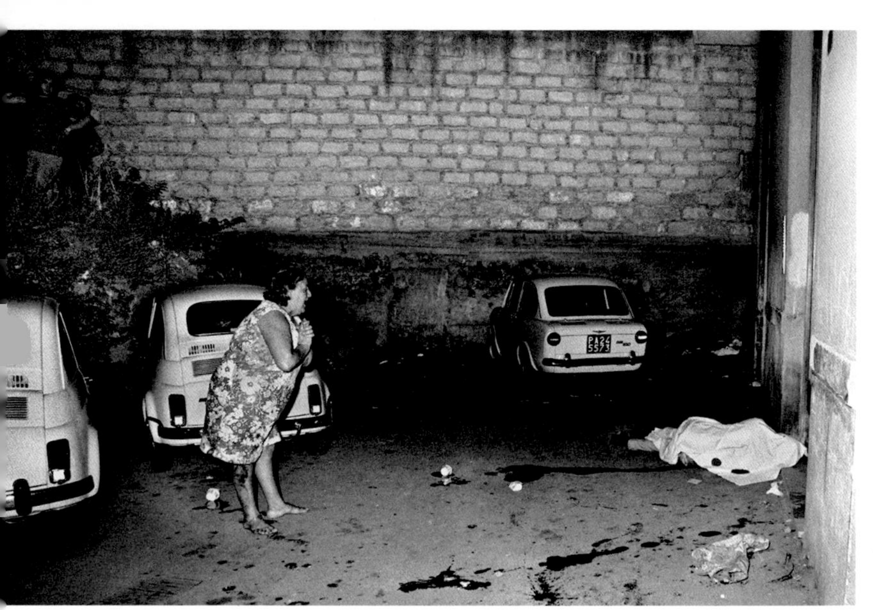

PA 24
5573

32. *He was killed on the way to the garage to get his car*, Palermo, 1976.

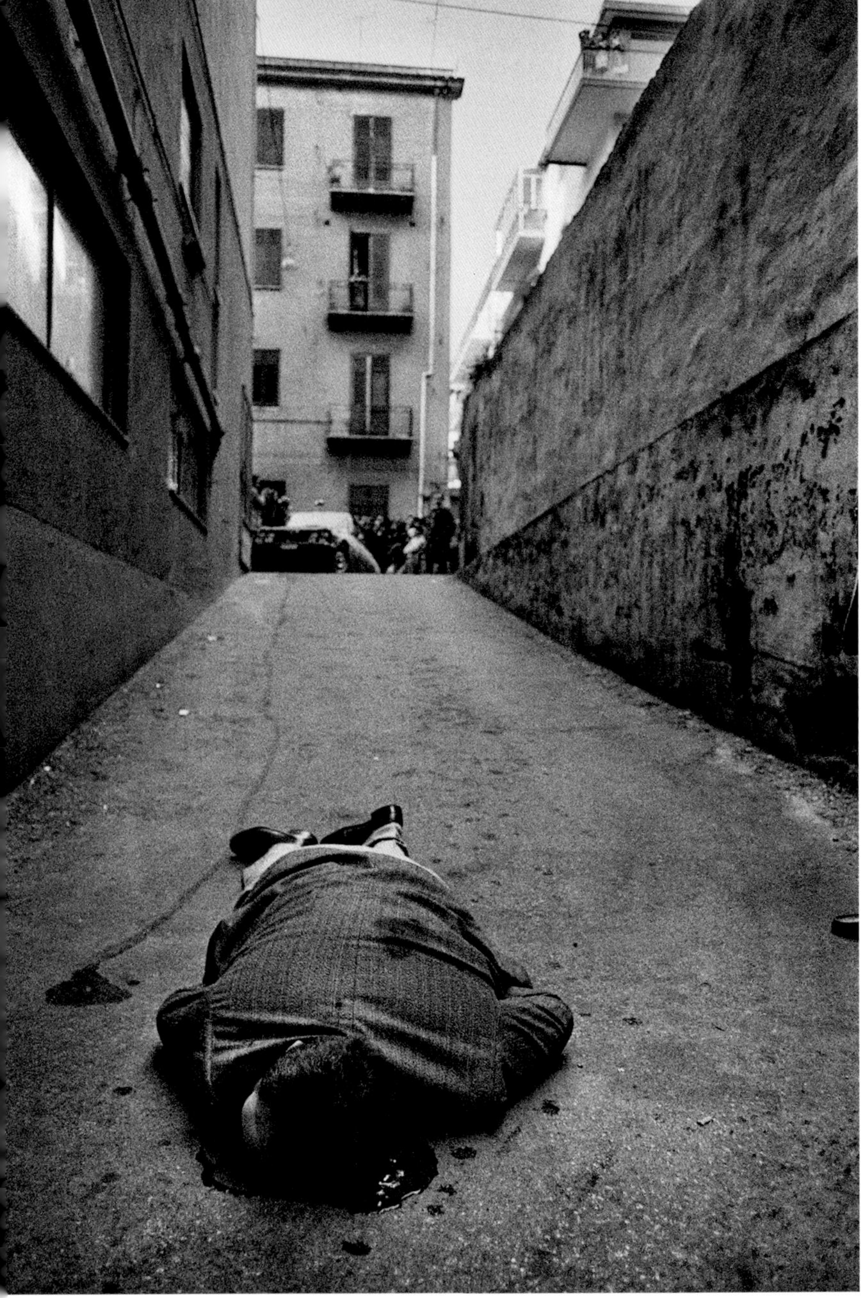

33. *Boris Giuliano, head of the Mobile Squad, on the crime scene in Piazza del Carmine*, Palermo, 1978.

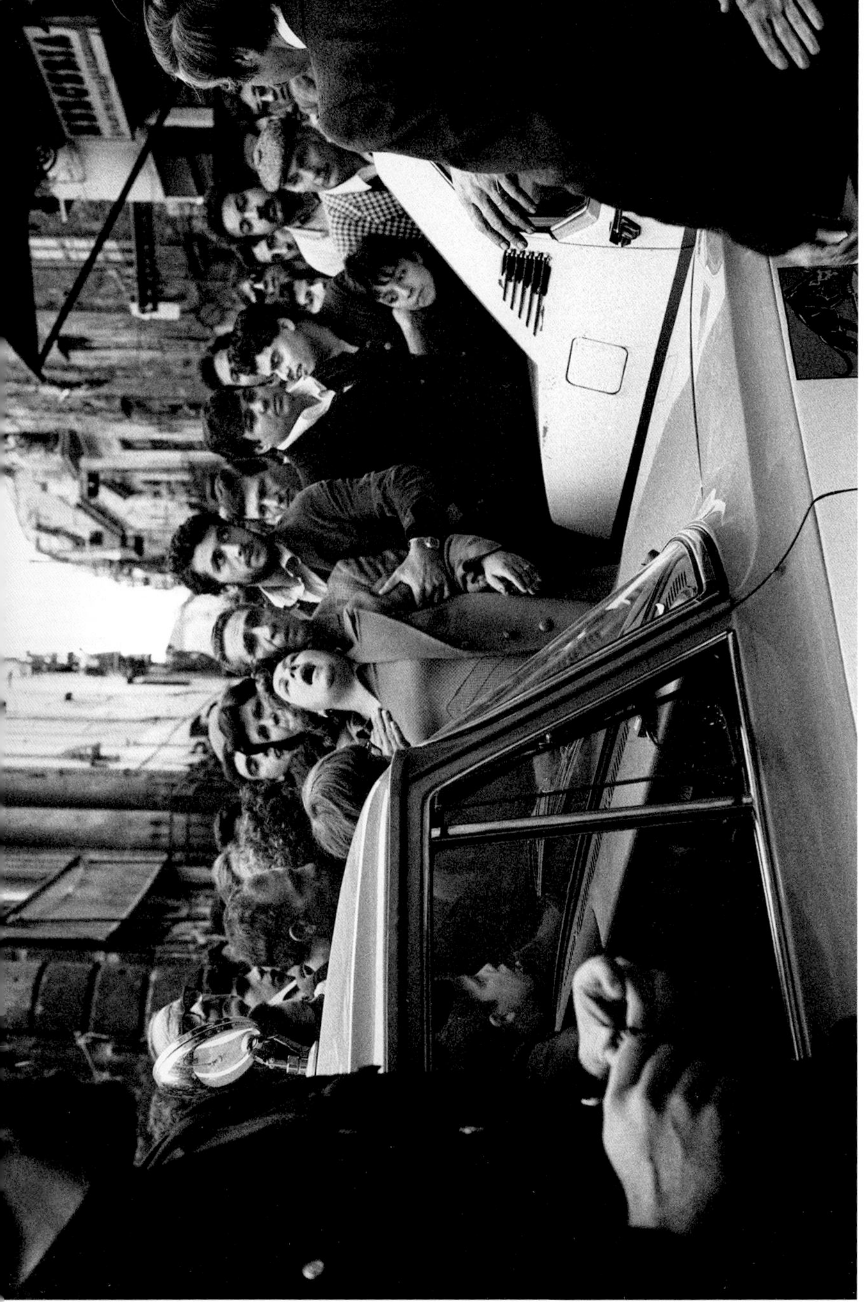

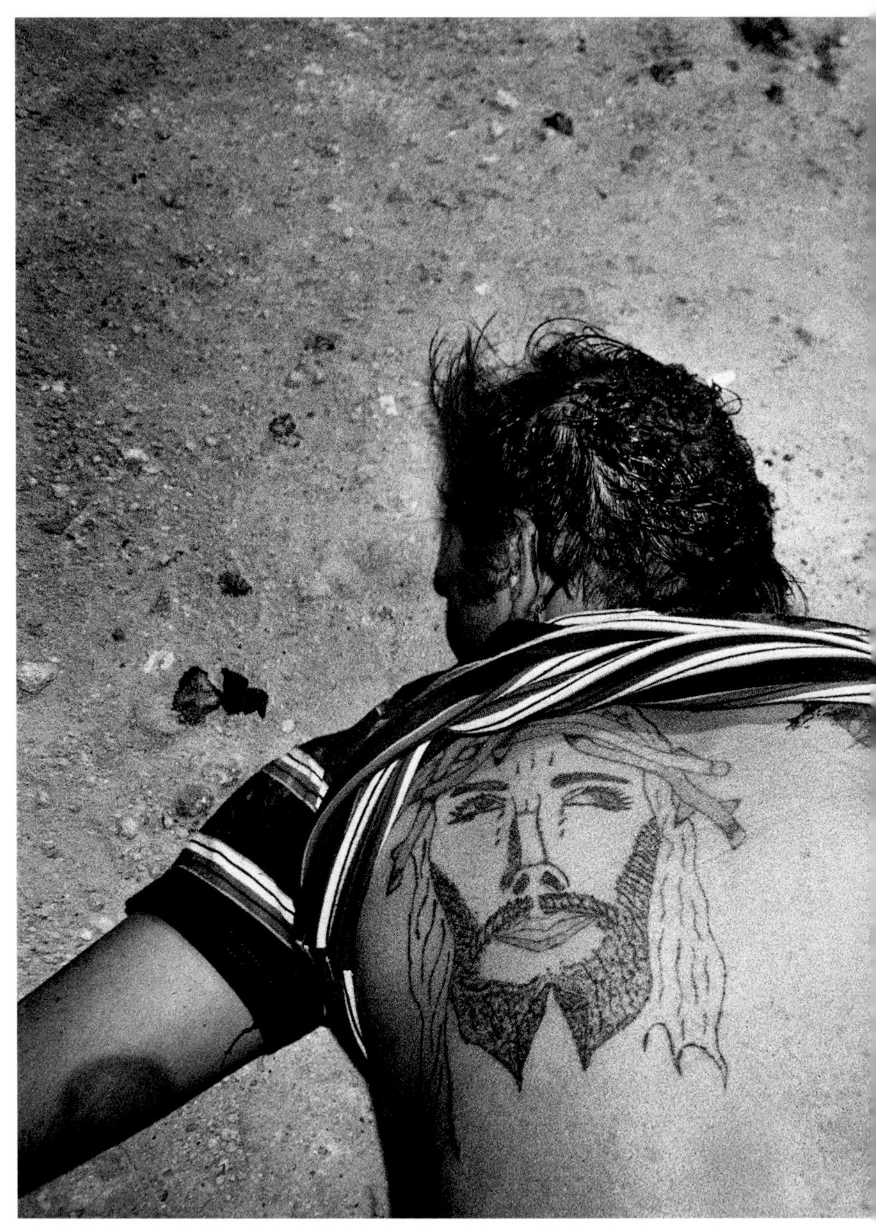

34. *The two Christs*, Palermo, 1982.

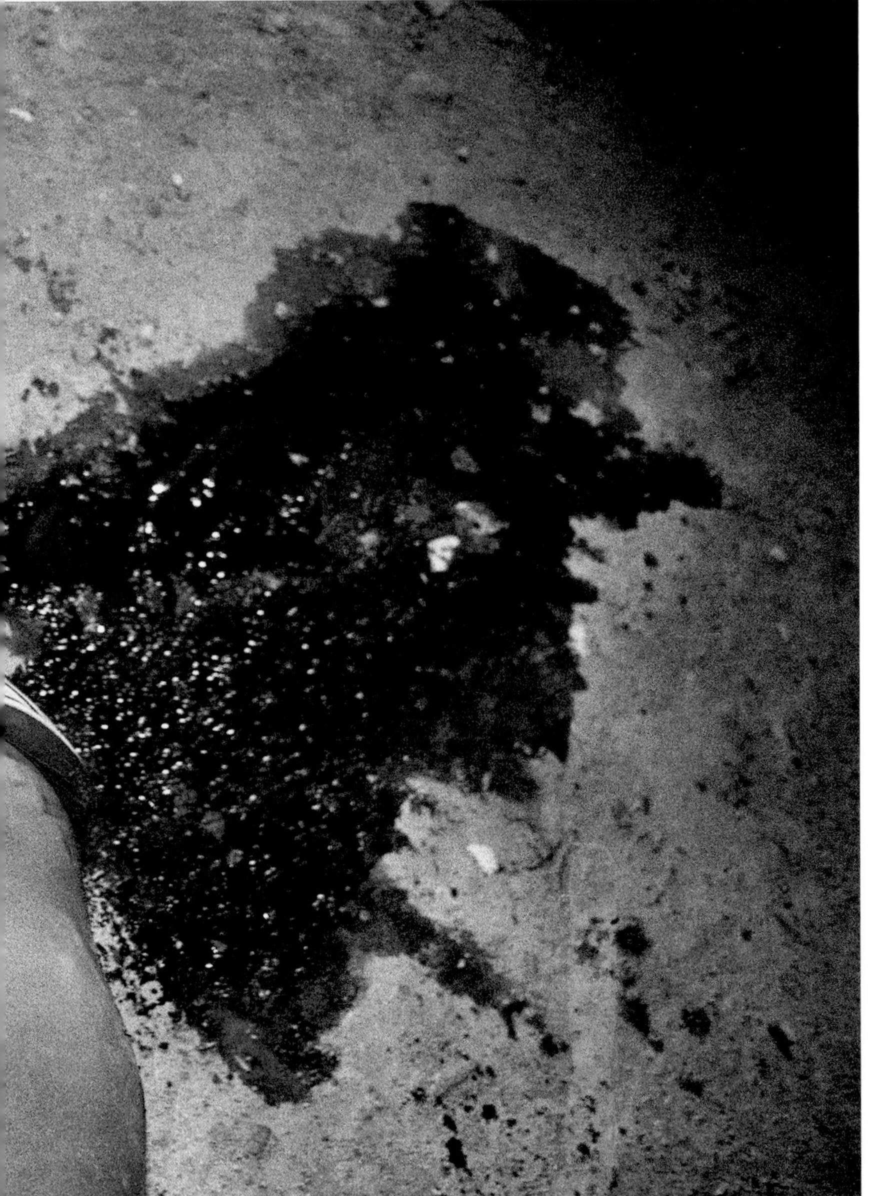

35. *Judge Cesare Terranova, Communist MP and member of the Parliamentary Anti-Mafia Commission, killed in an ambush. Marshal Lenin Mancuso, assigned to his surveillance, died shortly afterwards in hospital*, Palermo, 1979.

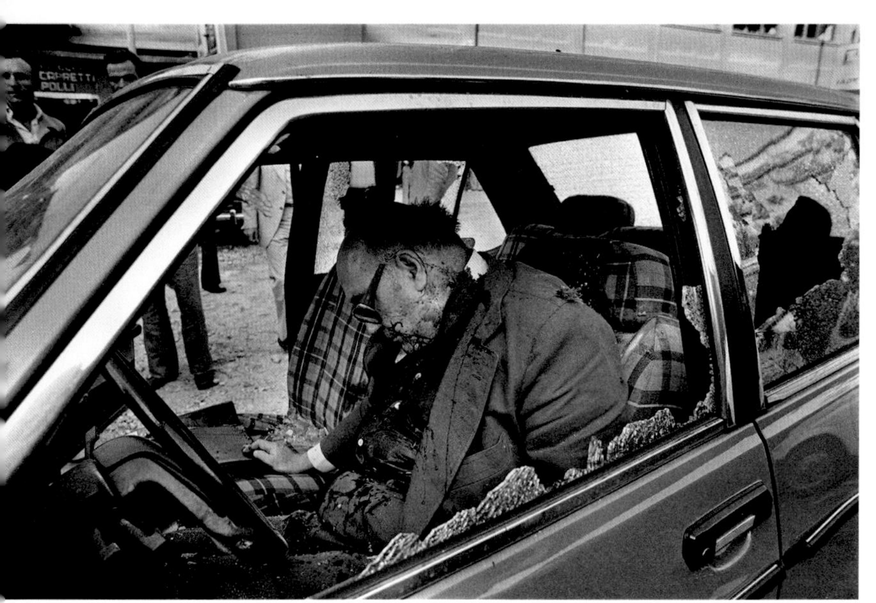

36. *The dry tree*, Palermo, 1984.

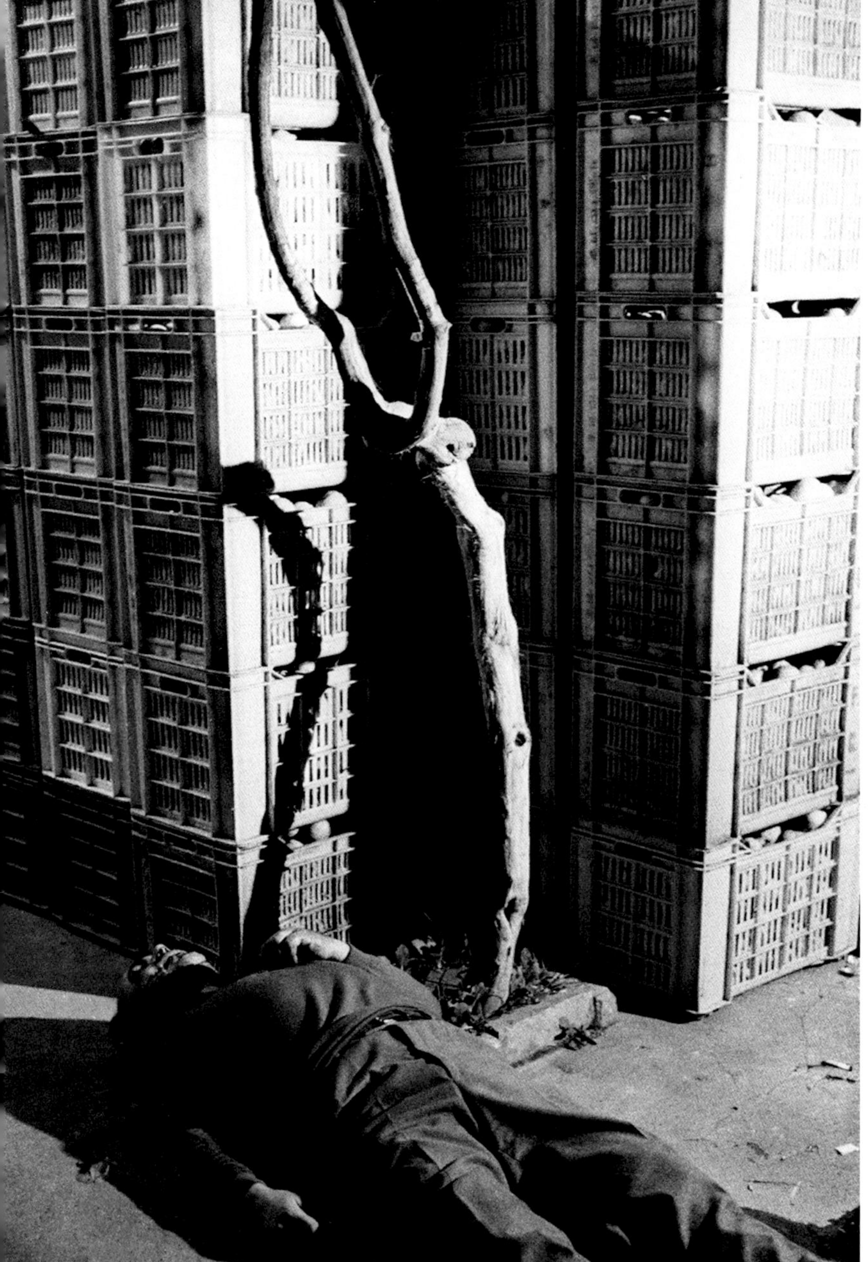

37. *La camera della morte*, Palermo, 1983.

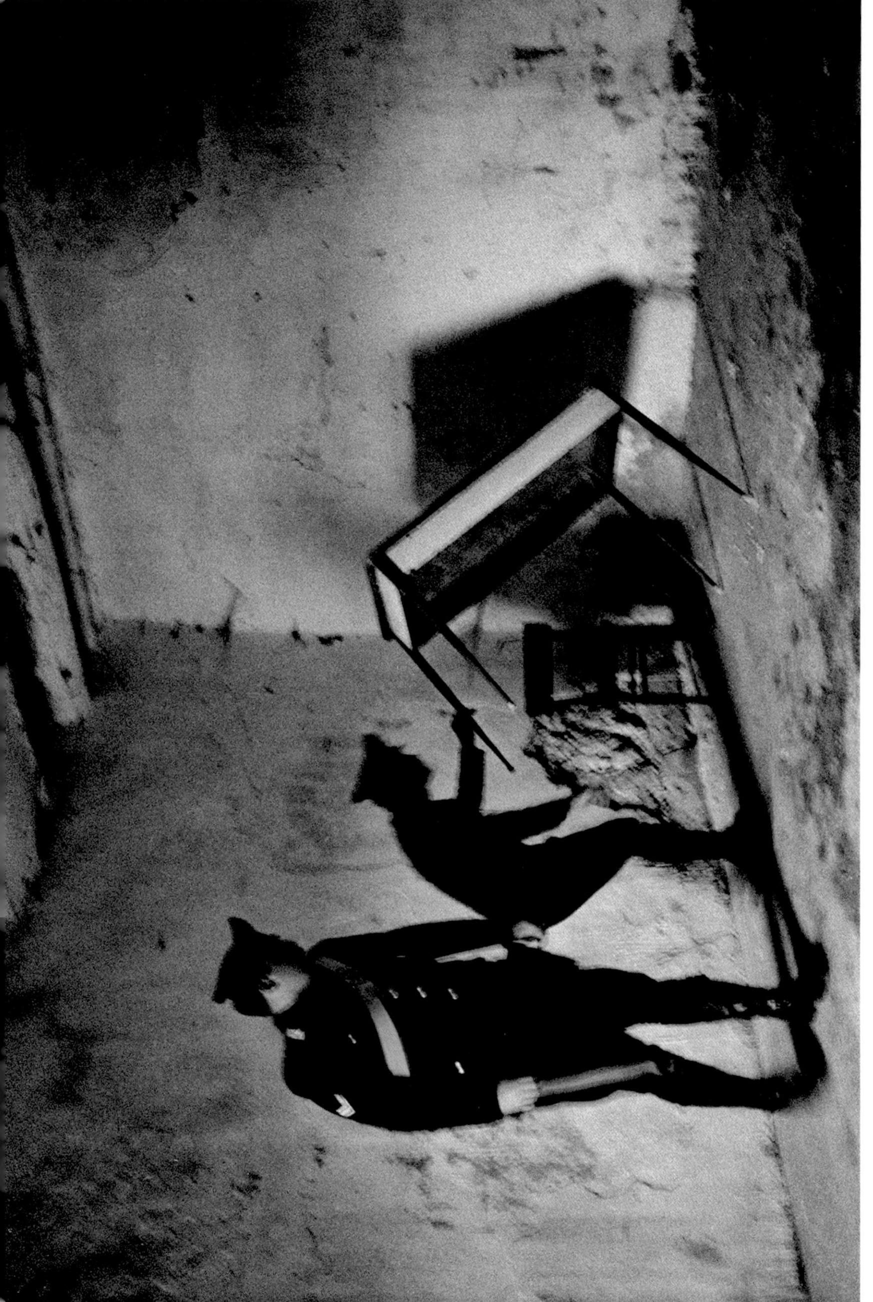

38. *A mother embraces her* carabiniere *son returning from a dangerous mission*, Palermo, 1979.

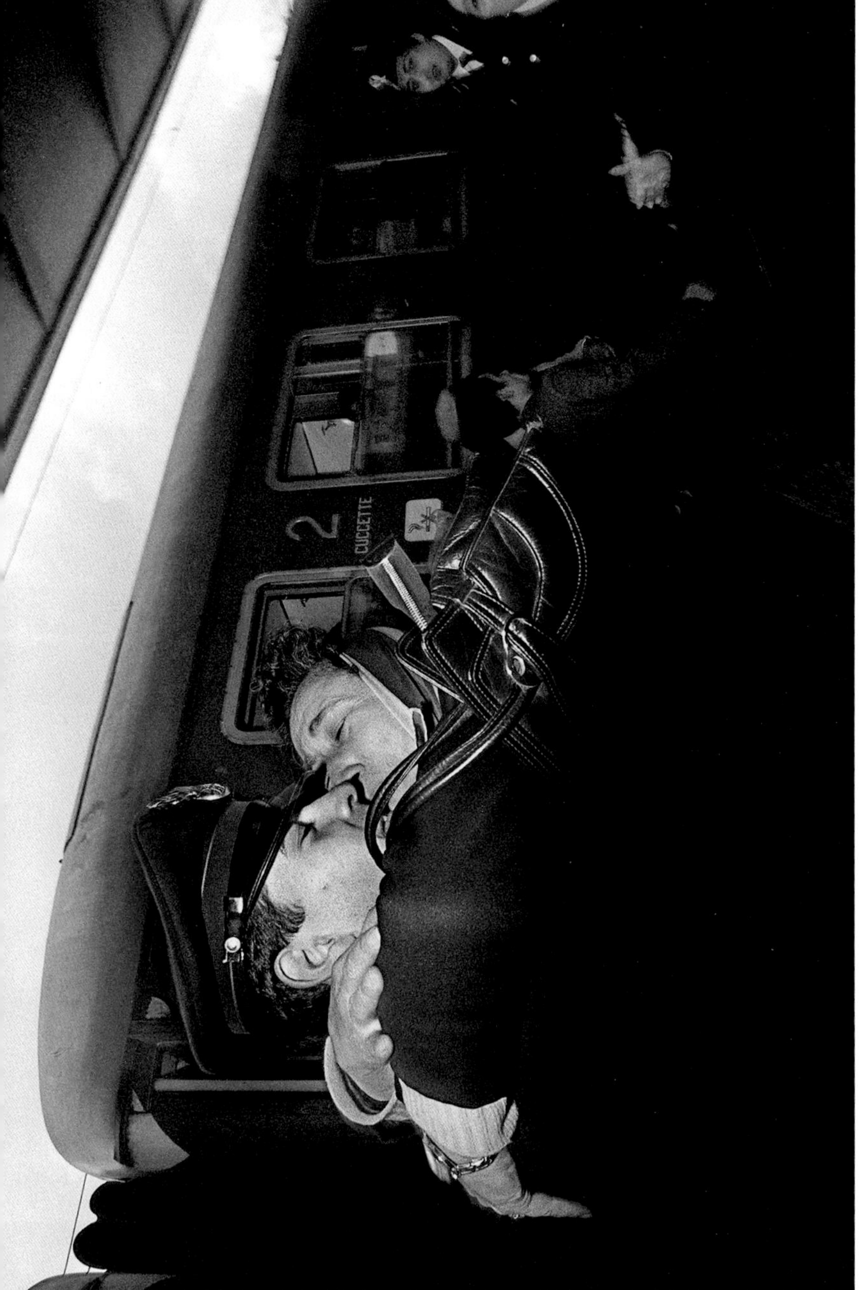

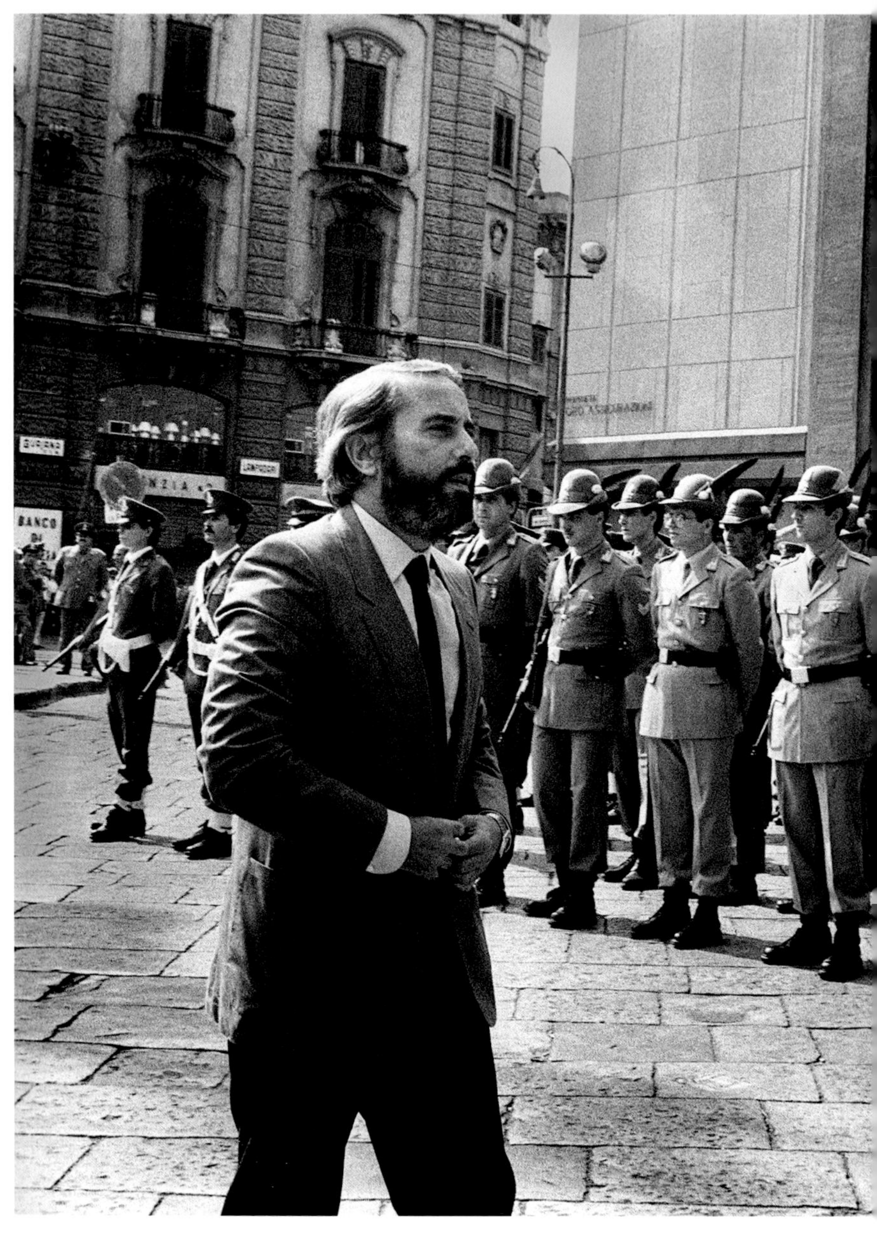

39. *Judge Giovanni Falcone at the funeral of*
General Carlo Alberto Dalla Chiesa, Palermo, 1982.

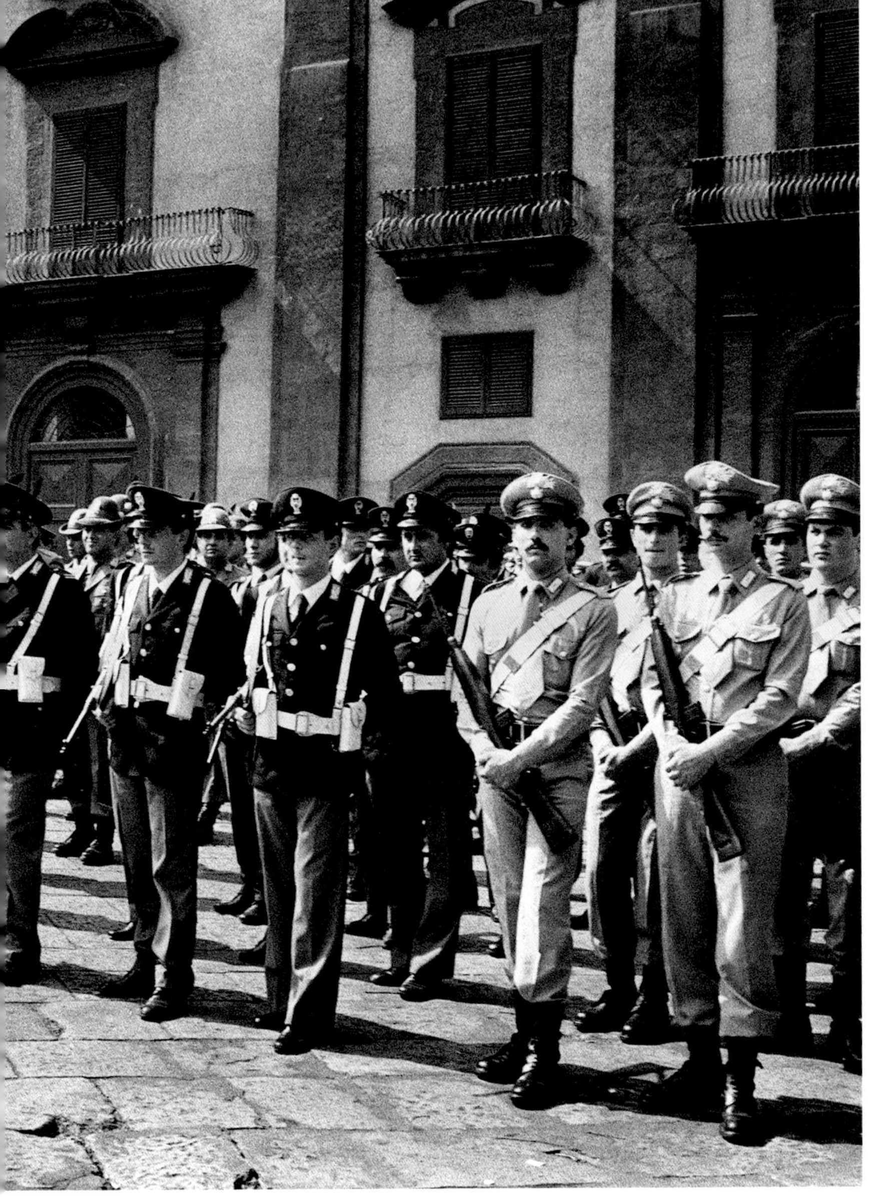

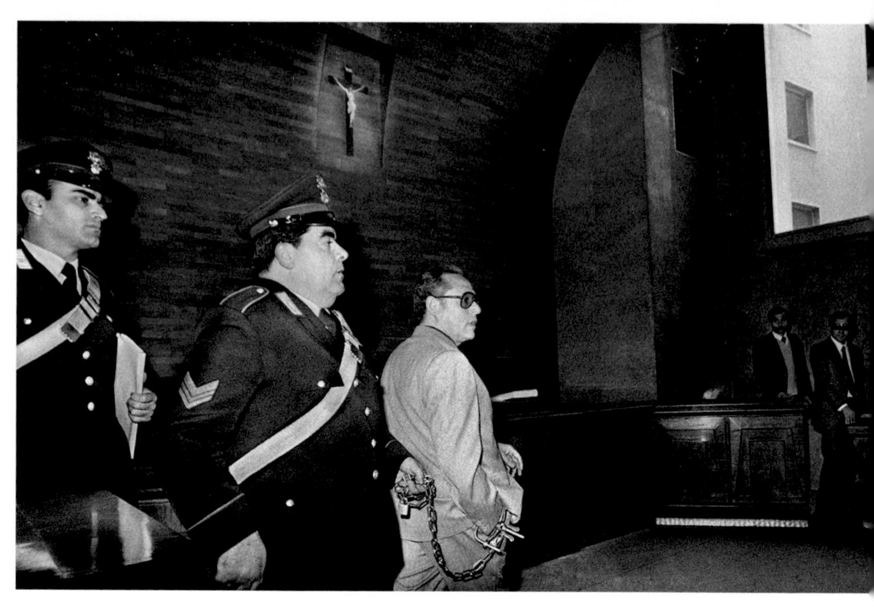

40. *Mafia boss Luciano Liggio in court*, Palermo, 1978.
41. *Giorgio Boris Giuliano, head of the Mobile Squad, on the crime scene of Lorenzo La Corte's homicide*, Palermo, 1975.

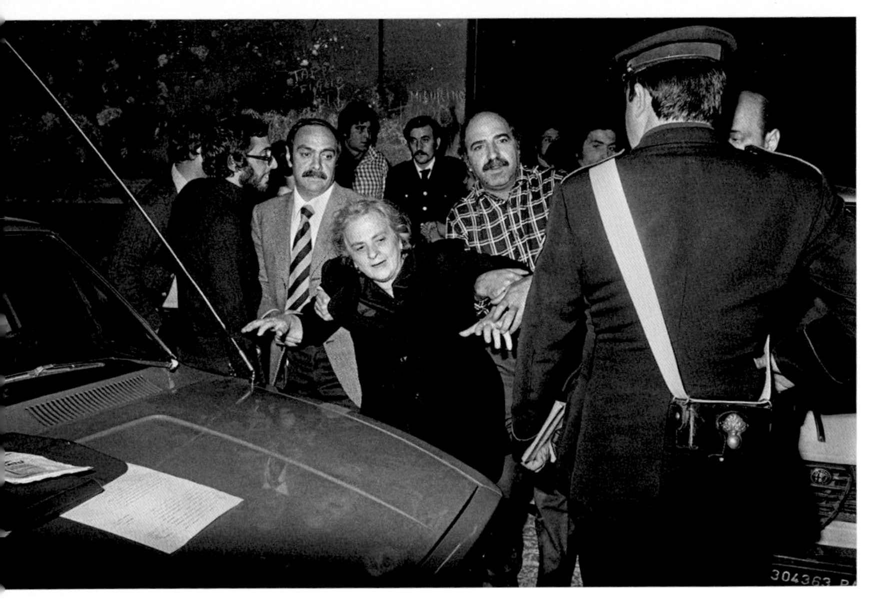

42. *The crowd observes the body of a young man killed in the Romagnolo neighbourhood. His twin brother will later also be assassinated*, Palermo, 1983.

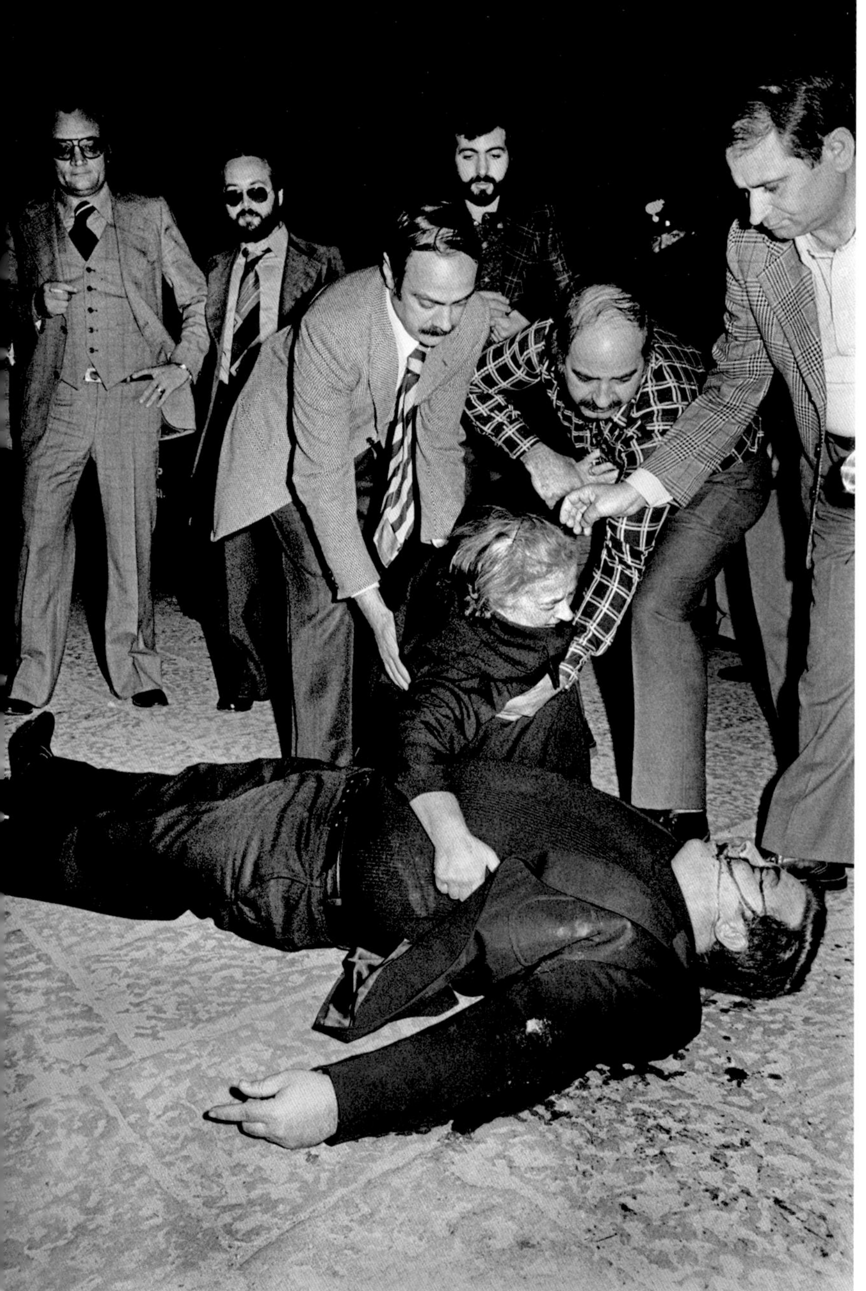

43. *Giorgio Boris Giuliano, head of the Mobile Squad, on the crime scene of Lorenzo La Corte's homicide*, Palermo, 1975.

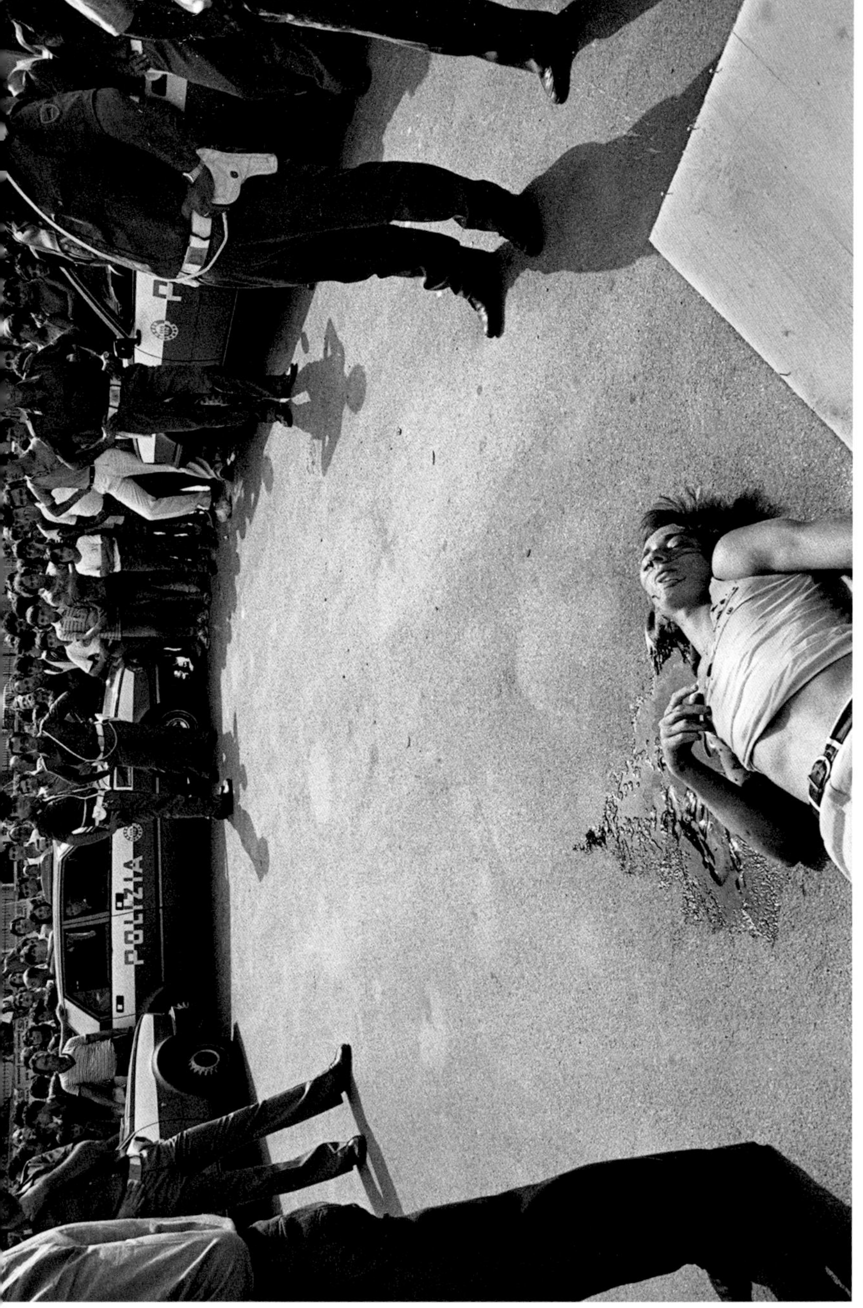

44. *President of the Sicilian region, Piersanti Mattarella, had just been shot by Mafia killers in front of his wife and daughter*, Palermo, 1980.

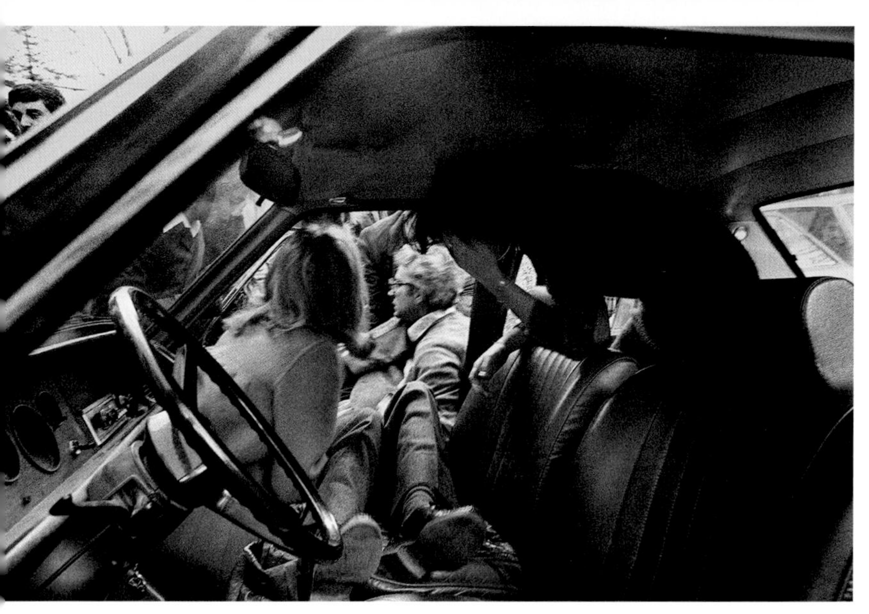

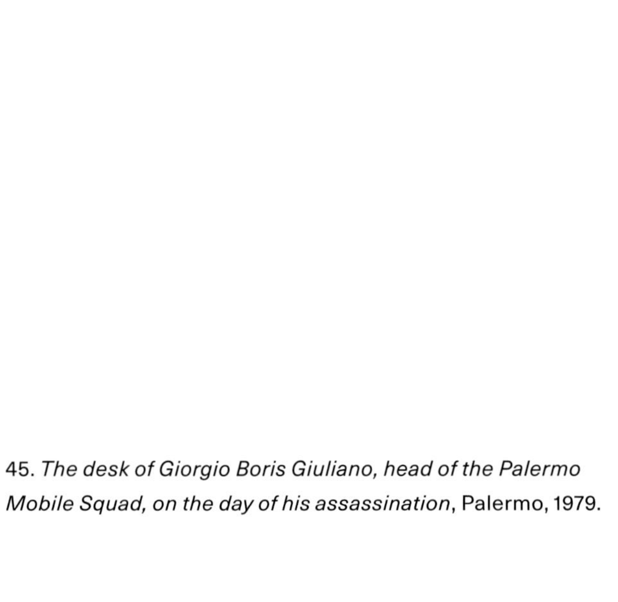

45. *The desk of Giorgio Boris Giuliano, head of the Palermo Mobile Squad, on the day of his assassination*, Palermo, 1979.

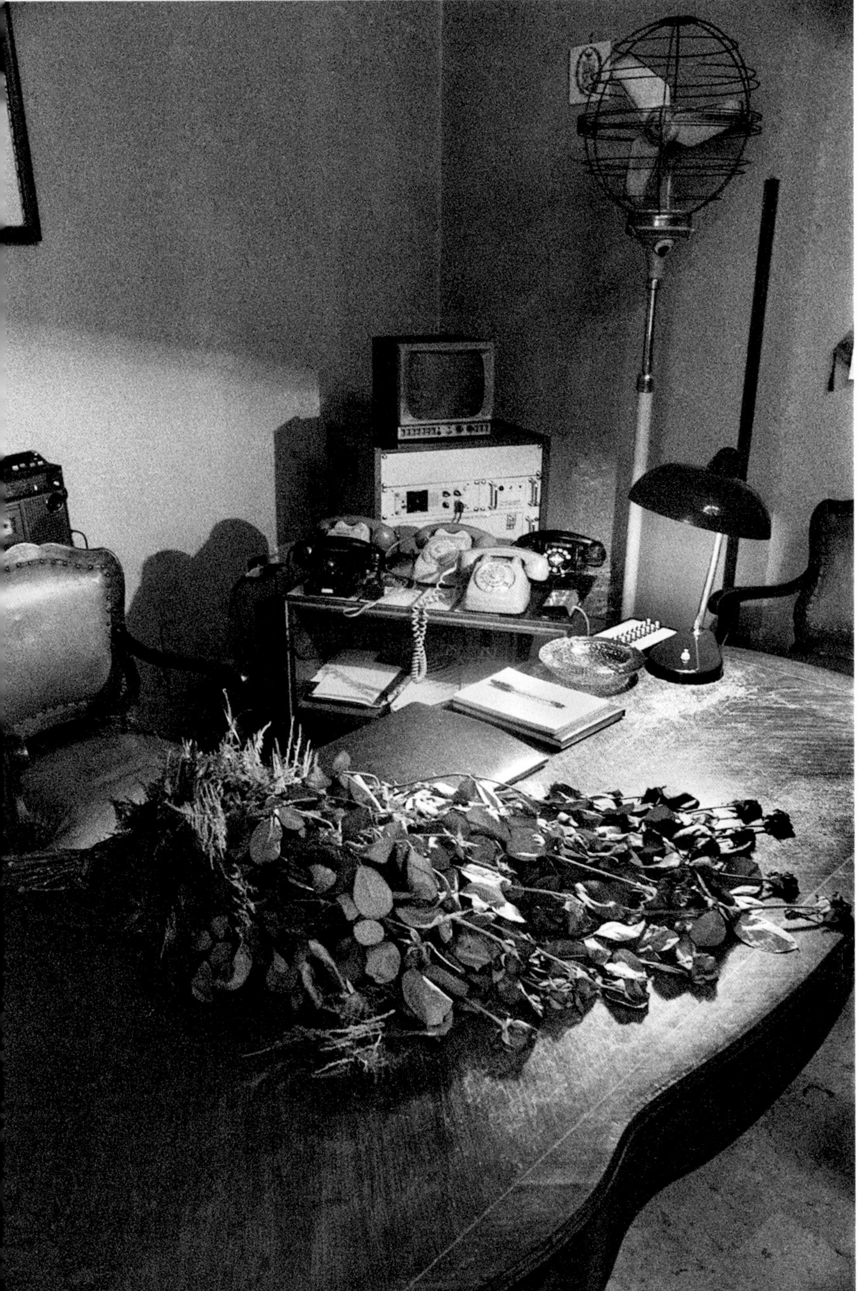

46. *Young journalist and Communist militant
Giuseppe Impastato, murdered by the Mafia*, Cinisi, 1978.

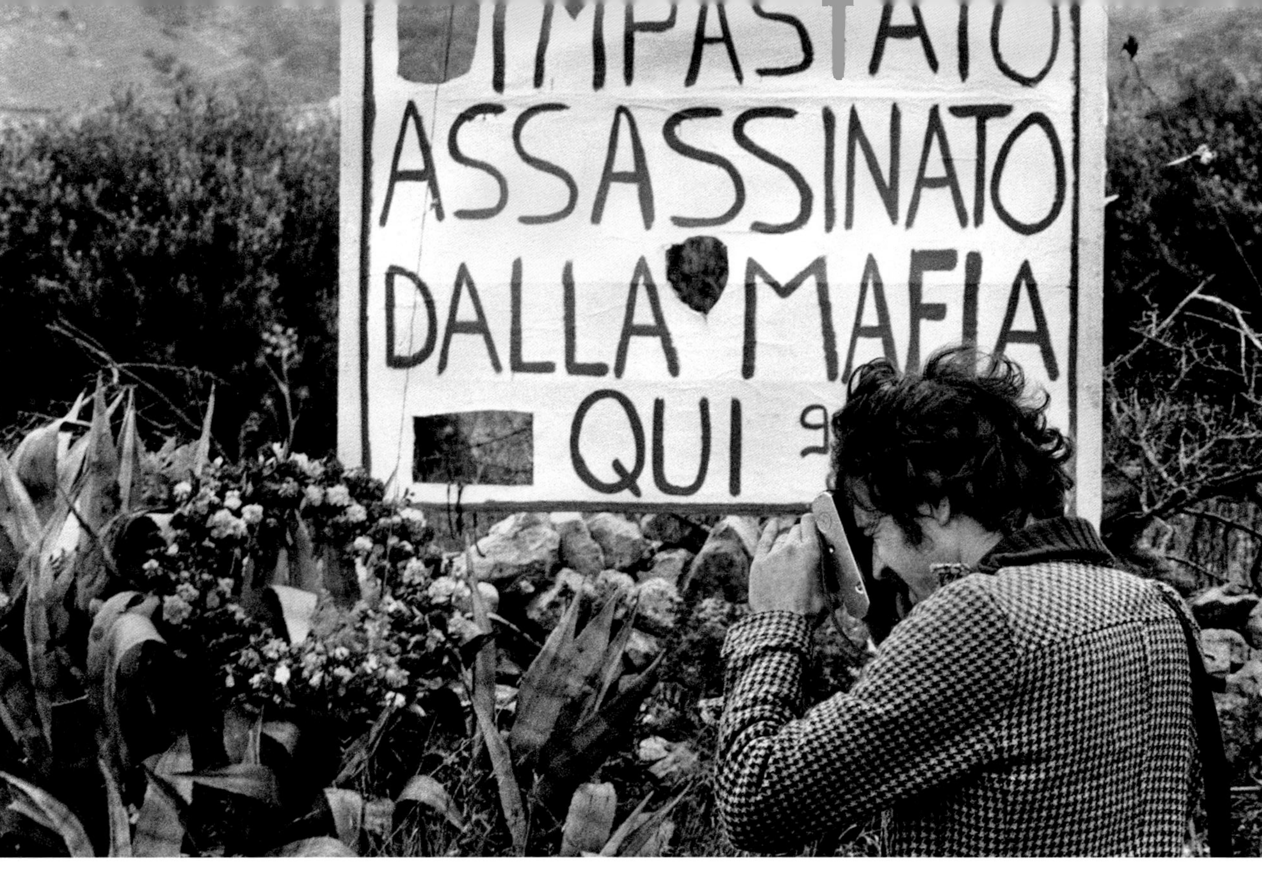

IMPASTATO
ASSASSINATO
DALLA MAFIA
QUI
9

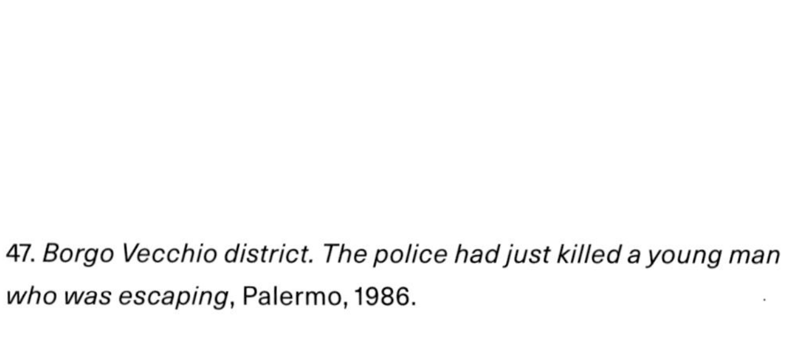

47. *Borgo Vecchio district. The police had just killed a young man who was escaping*, Palermo, 1986.

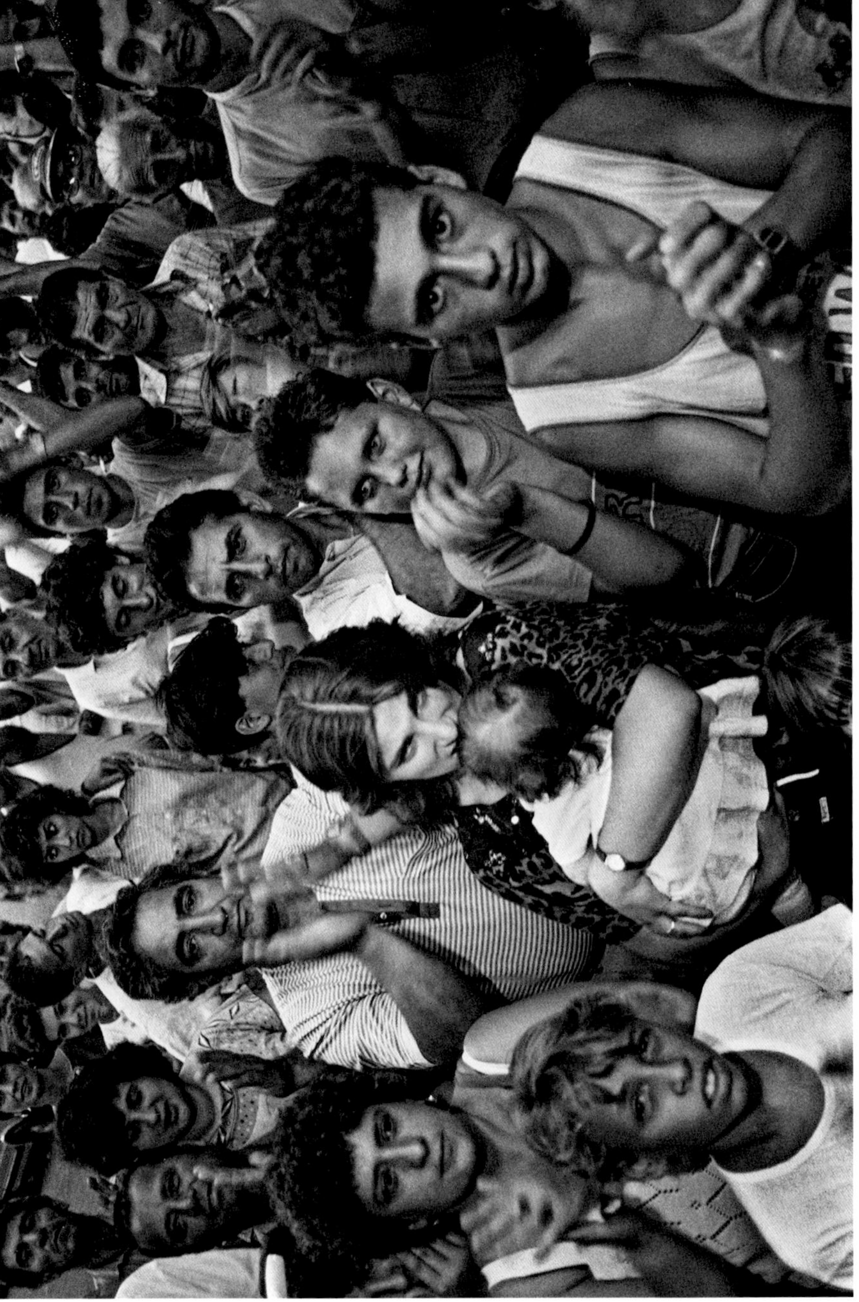

48. *Prisoners behind bars at the Ucciardone prison*, Palermo, 1983.

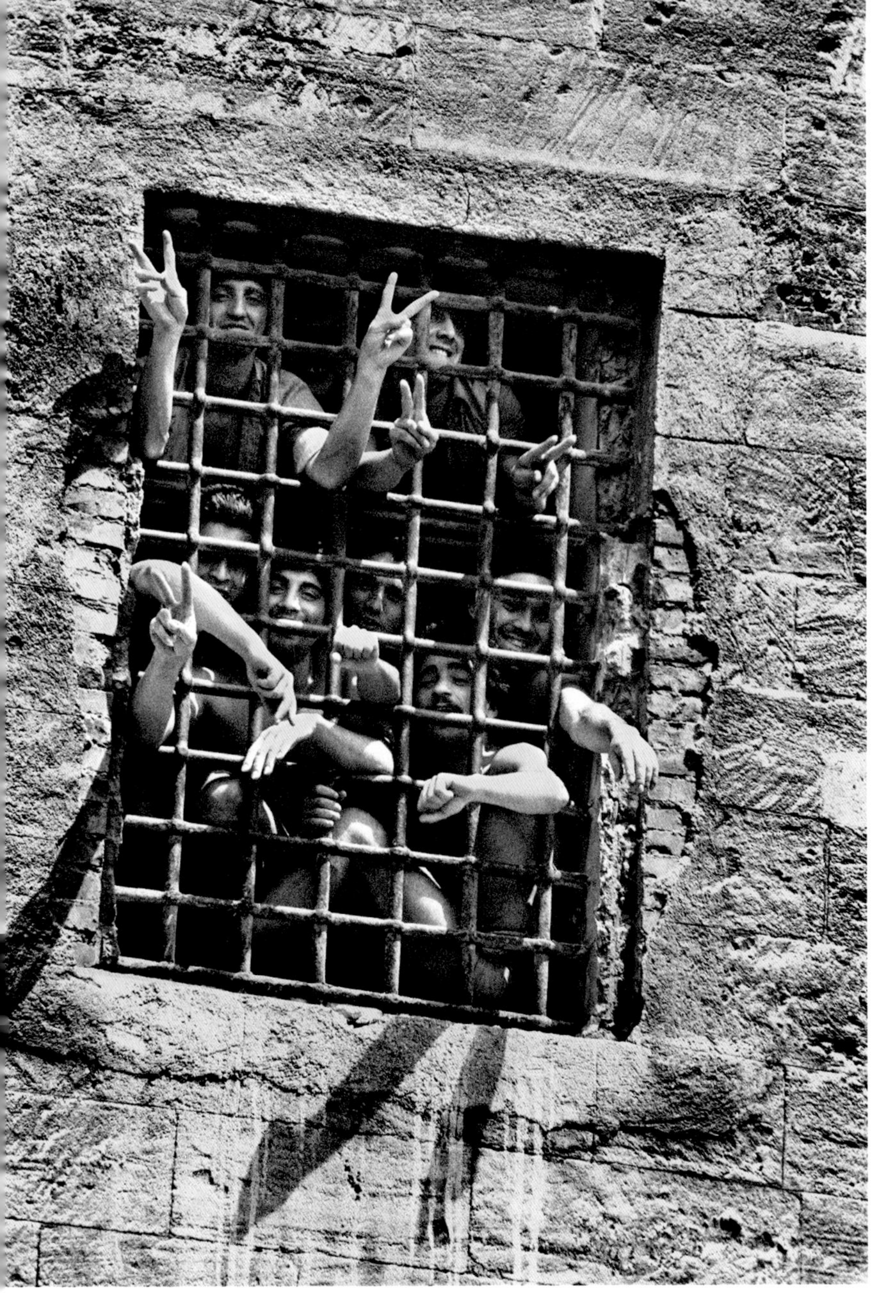

49. *Giulio Andreotti with the mafioso Nino Salvo and other politicians at the Zagarella Hotel*, Santa Flavia, 1978.

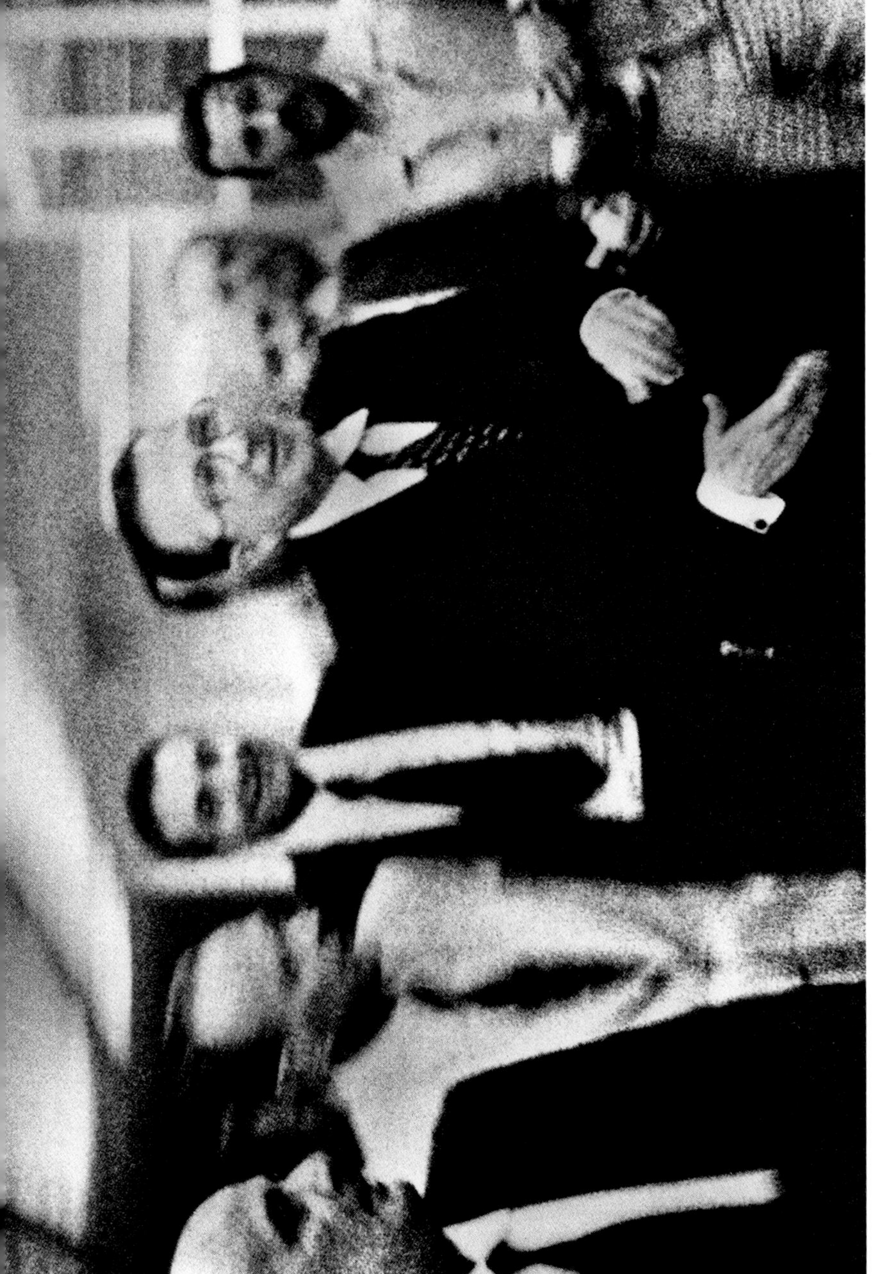

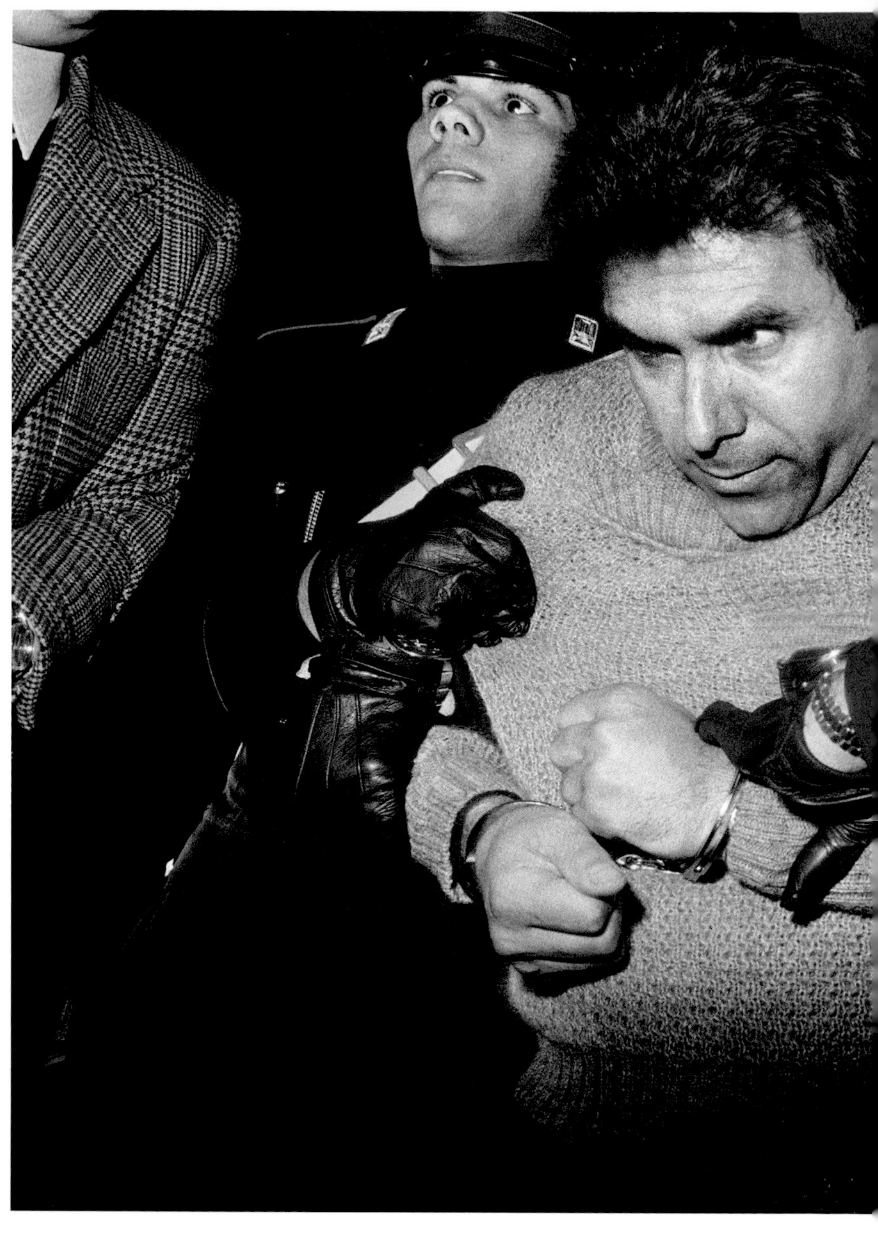

50. *The arrest of ferocious Mafia boss Leoluca Bagarella*, Palermo, 1979.

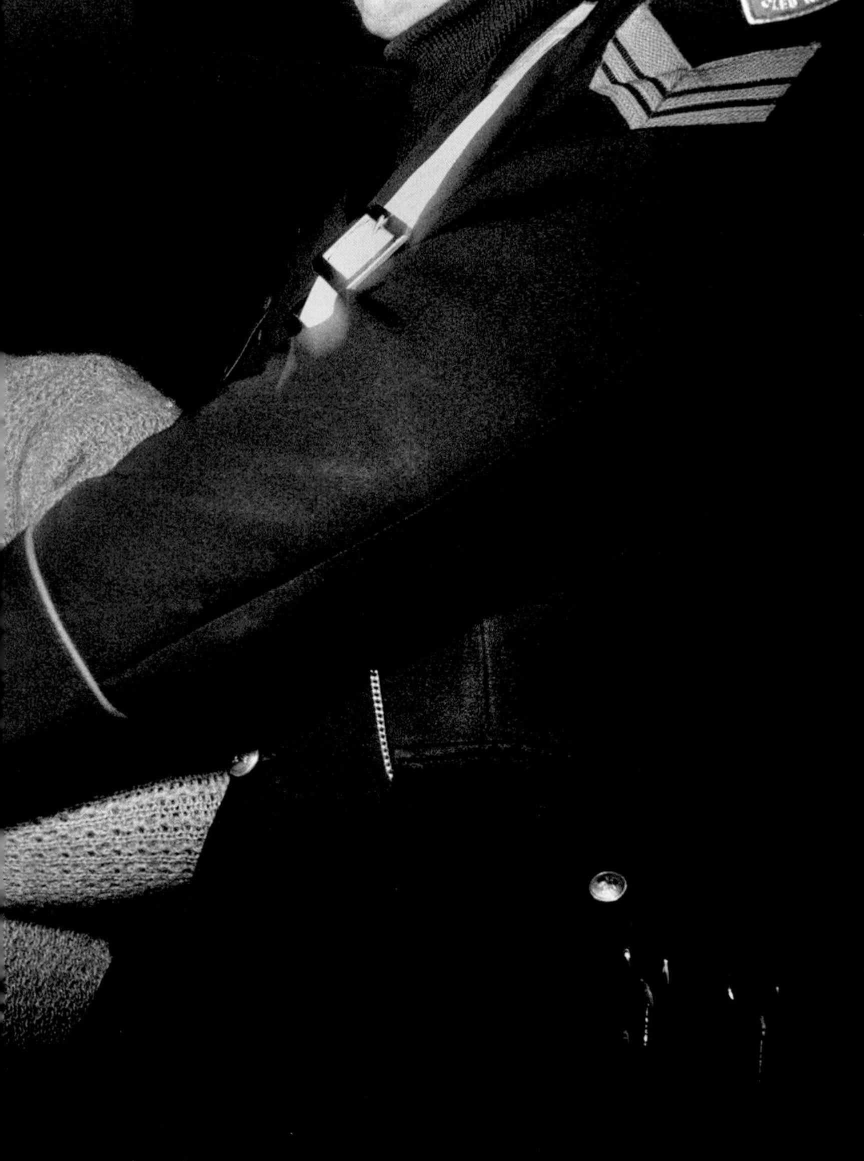

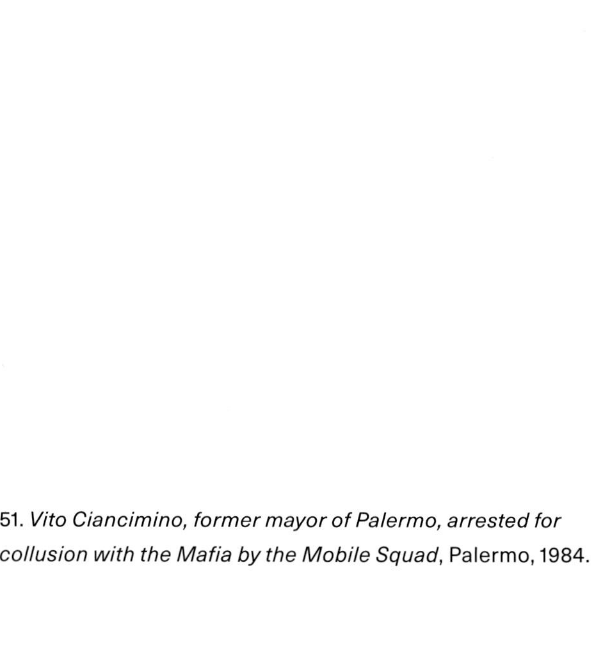

51. *Vito Ciancimino, former mayor of Palermo, arrested for collusion with the Mafia by the Mobile Squad*, Palermo, 1984.

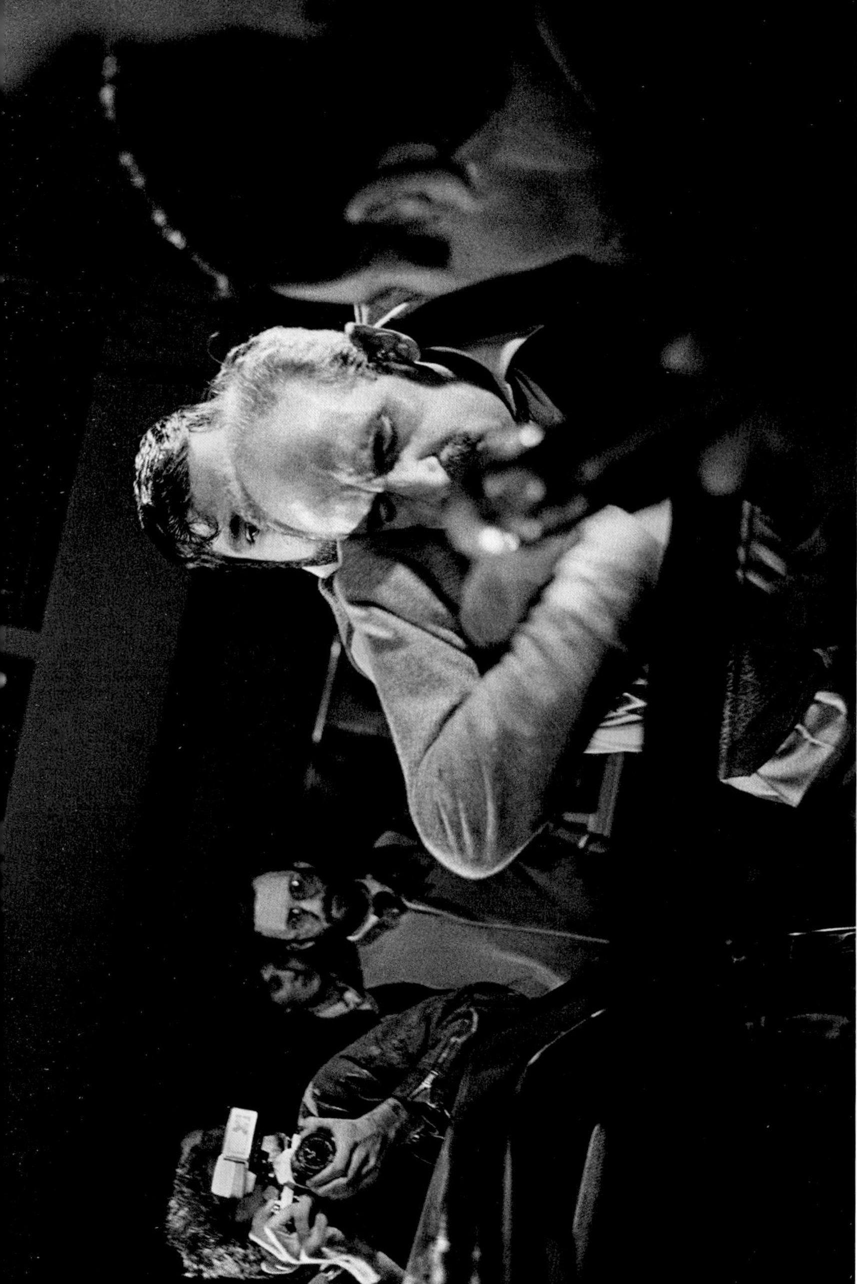

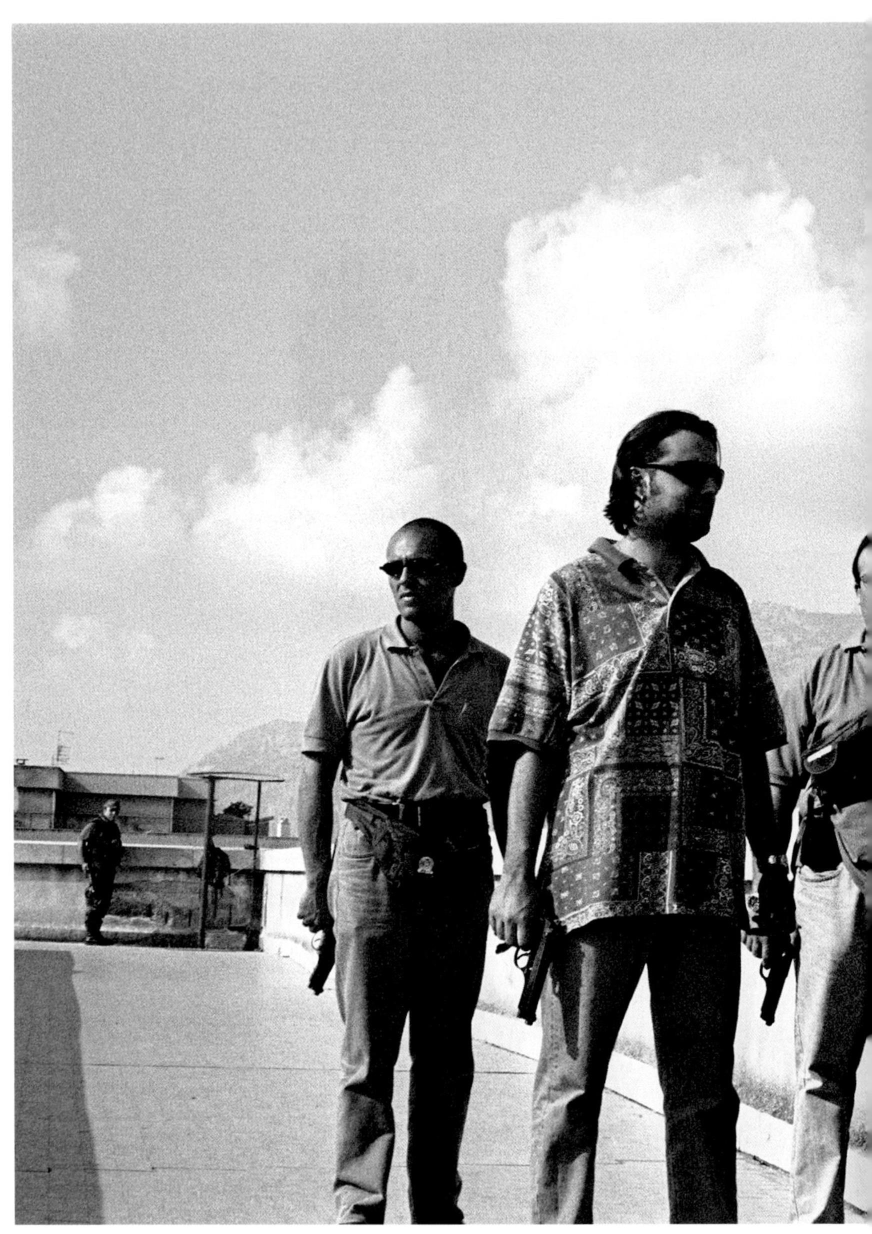

52. *Magistrate Roberto Scarpinato with his escort
on the roofs of the court*, Palermo, 1998.

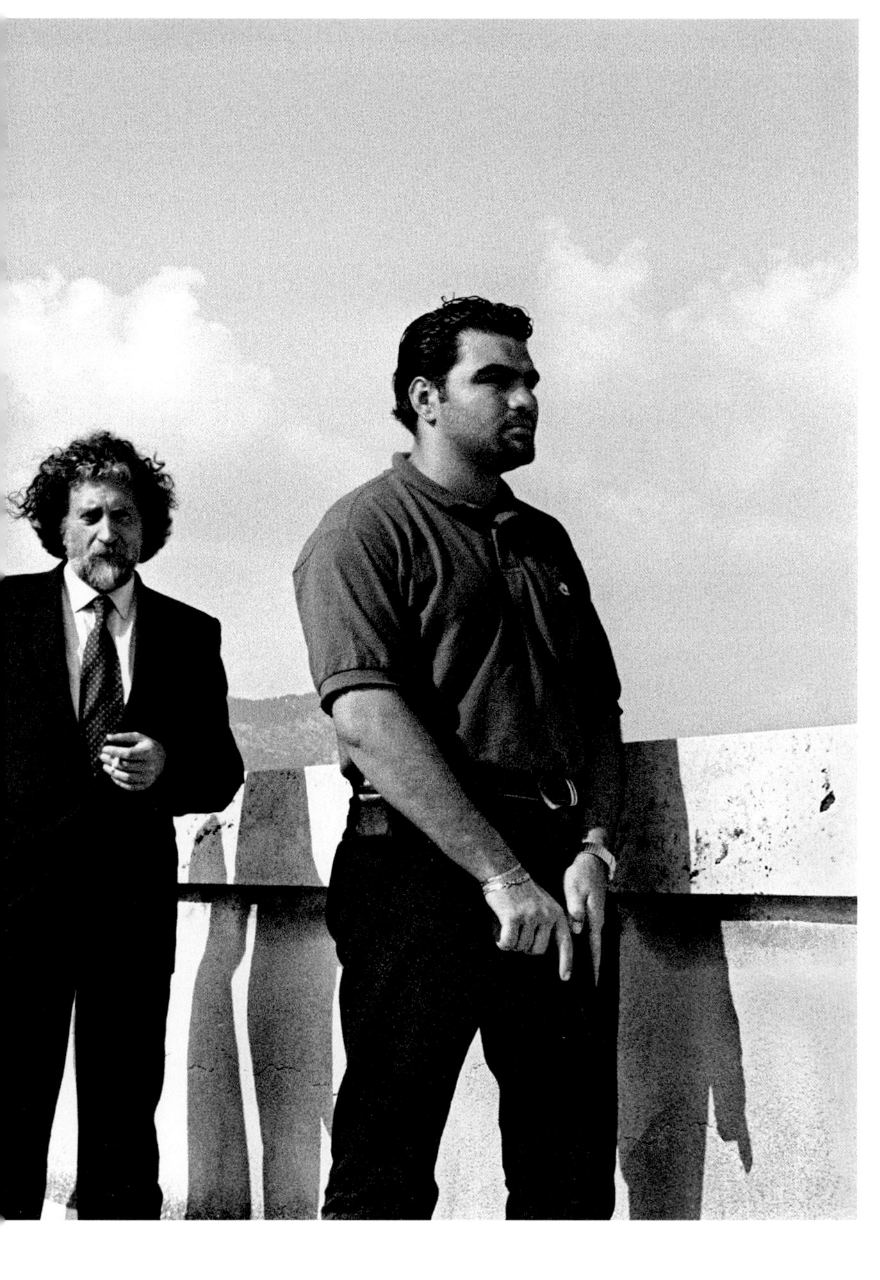

53. *Triple homicide at the Vucciria*, Palermo, 1978.

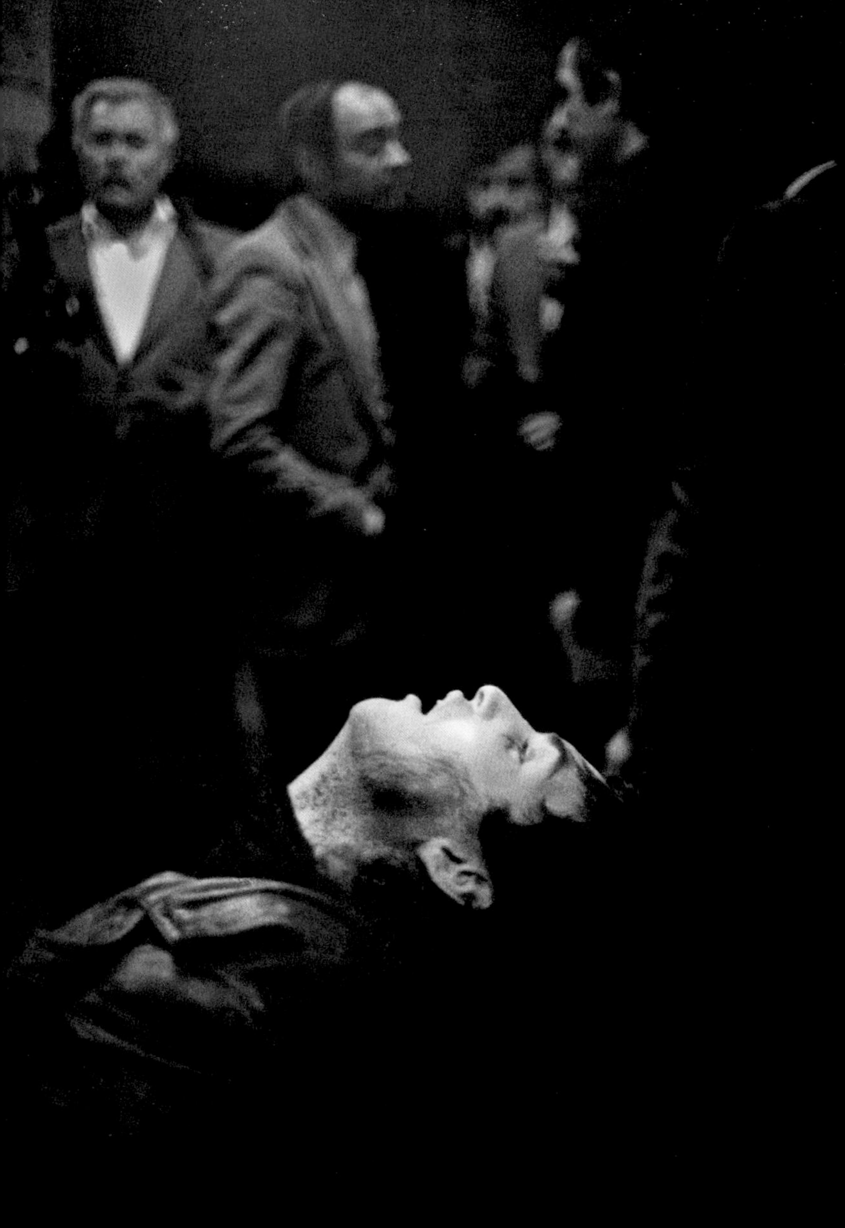

54. Rosaria Schifani, widow of the bodyguard Vito, killed together with Judge Giovanni Falcone, Francesca Morvillo and their colleagues Antonio Montinaro and Rocco Dicillo, Palermo, 1992.

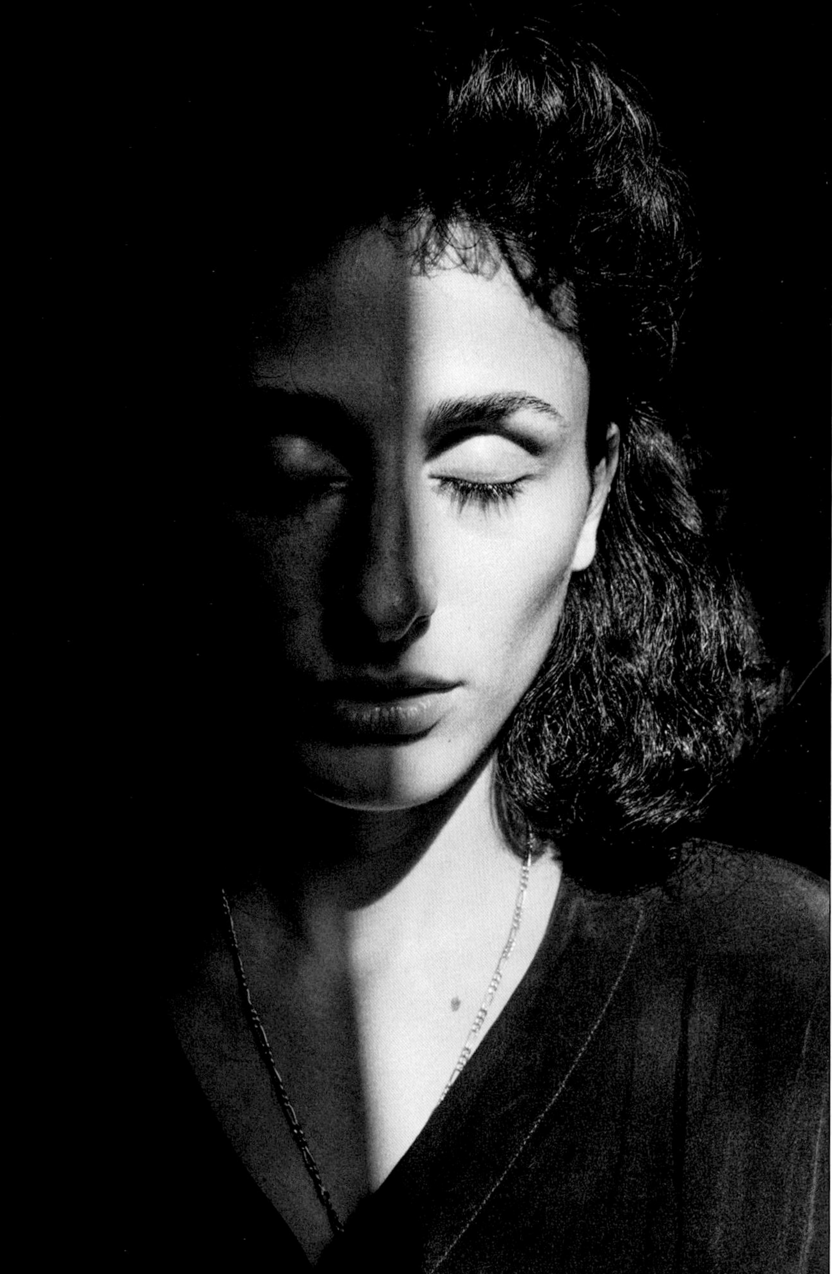

55. *Feast of San Giuliano*, Pollina, 1986.

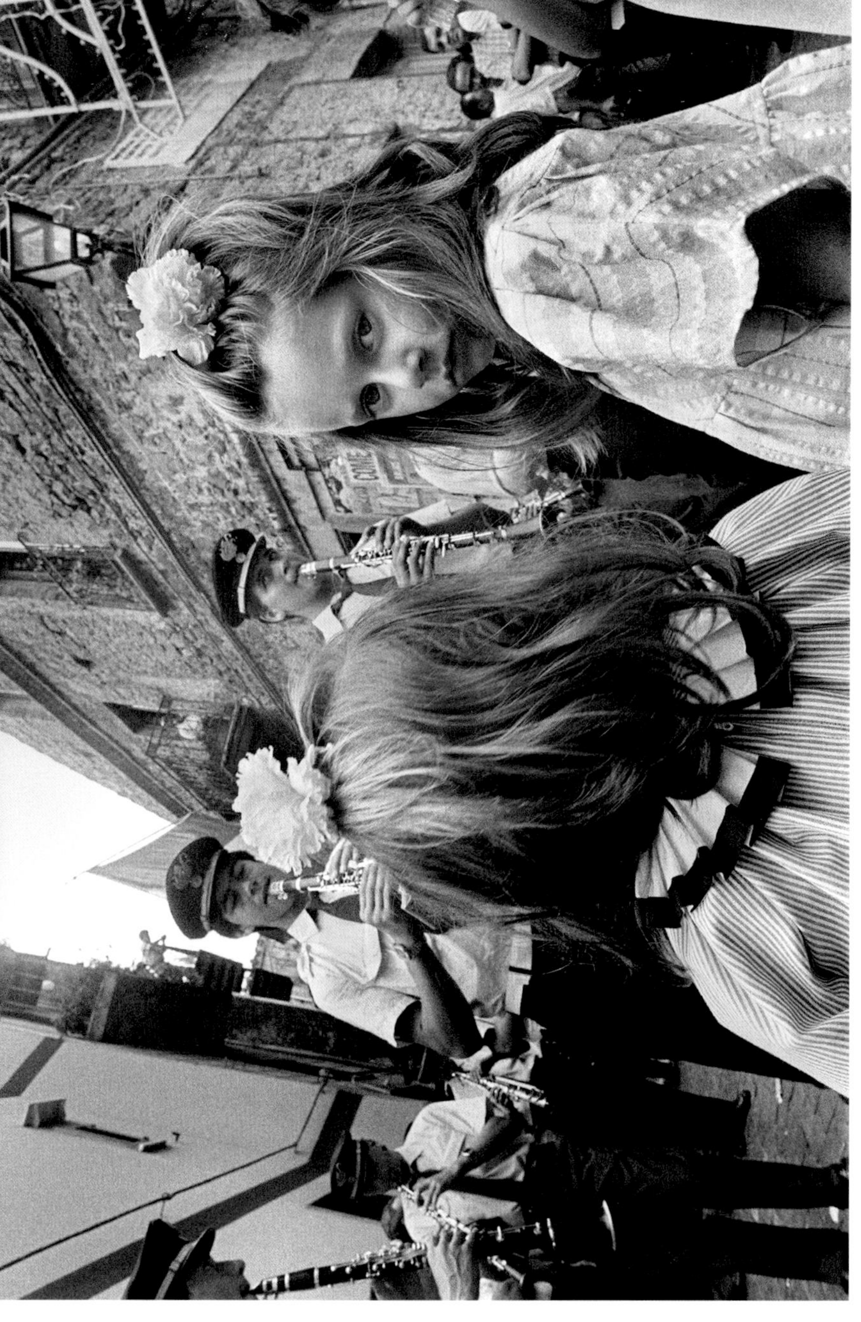

56. *Hooded man before the procession*, Enna, 1984.

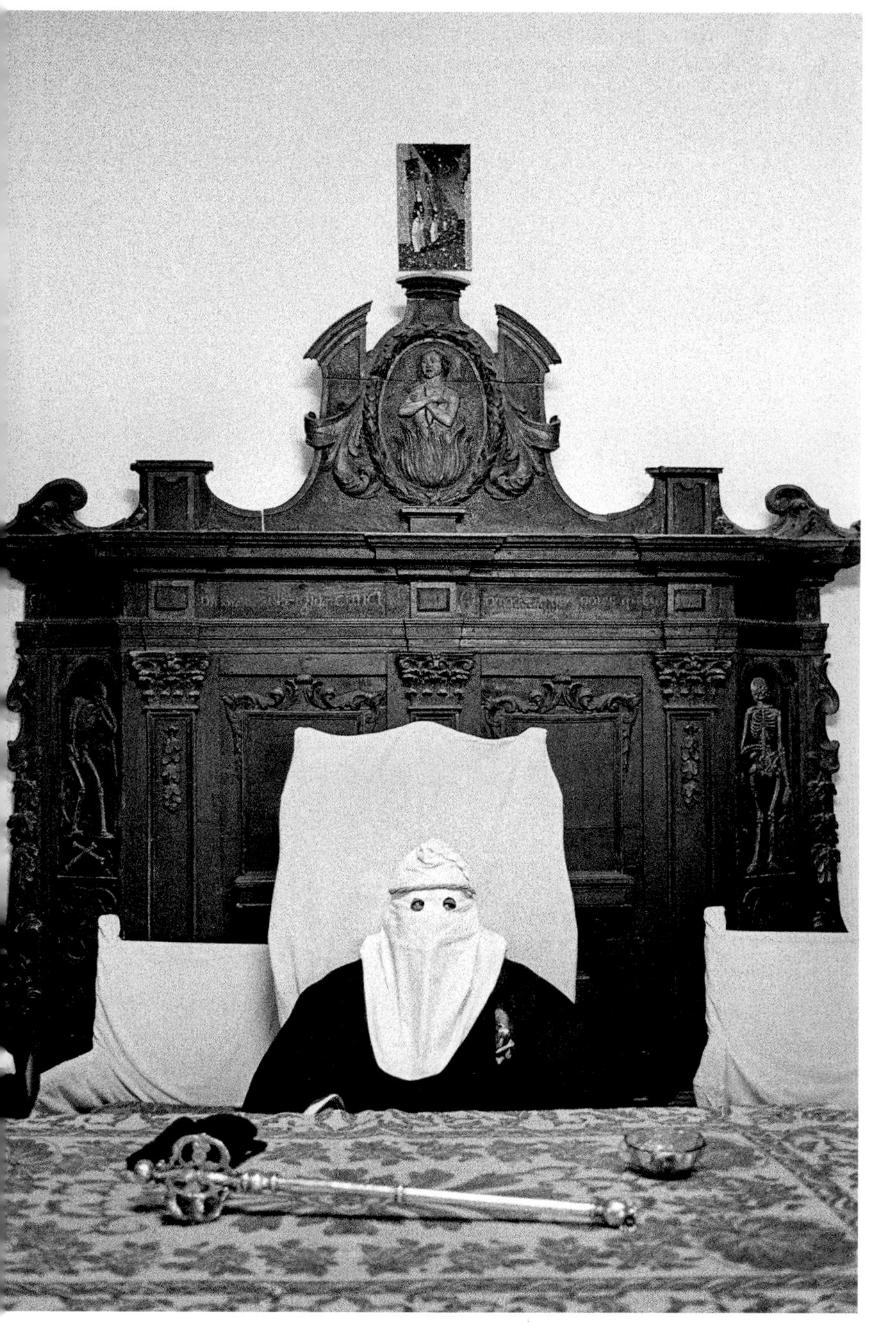

57. *San Giusto celebration. The horse broke its leg during the race. It will be put down later the same day. Meanwhile, the race continues*, Misilmeri, 1981.

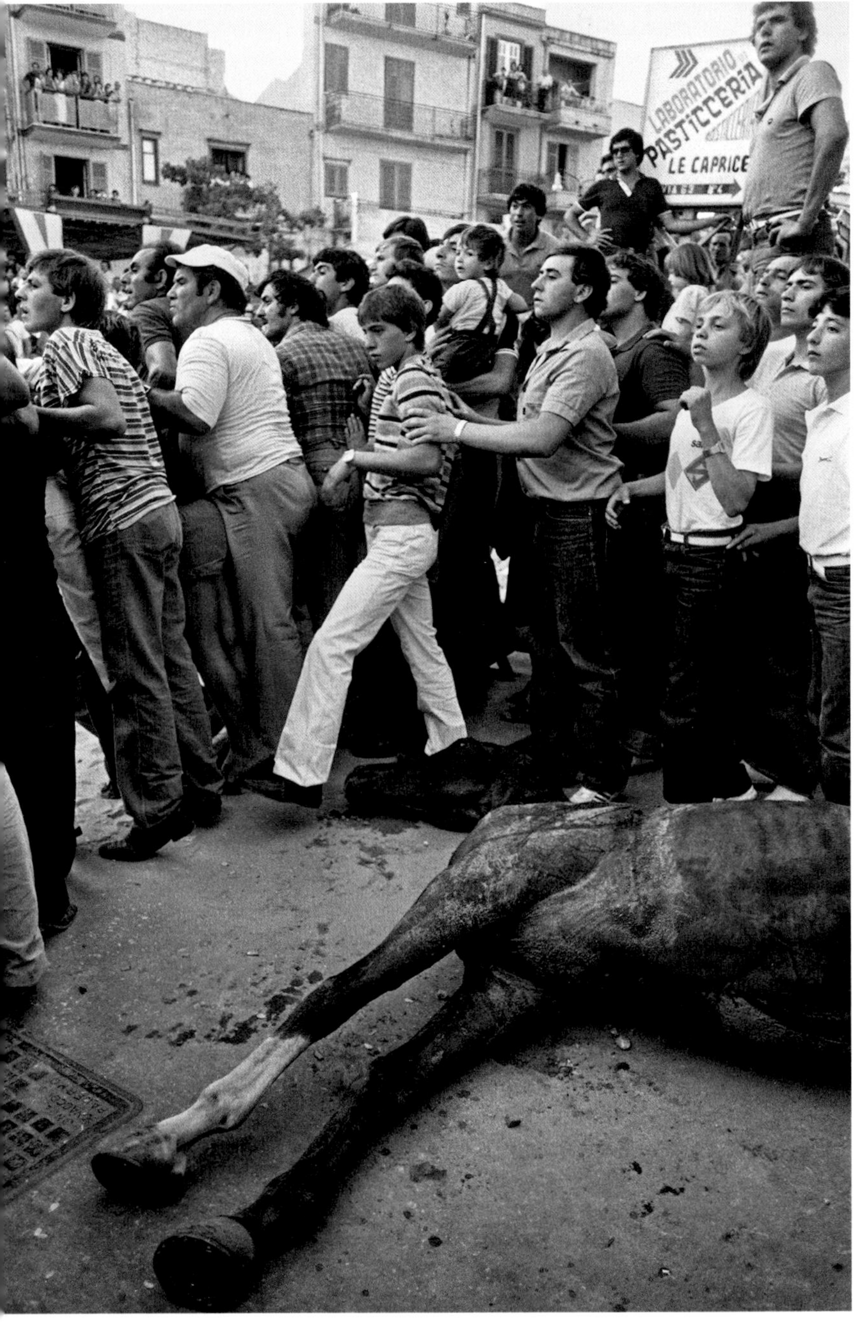

LABORATORIO DI
PASTICCERIA
LE CAPRICE

58. *The Procession of the Mysteries*, Collesano, 1985.

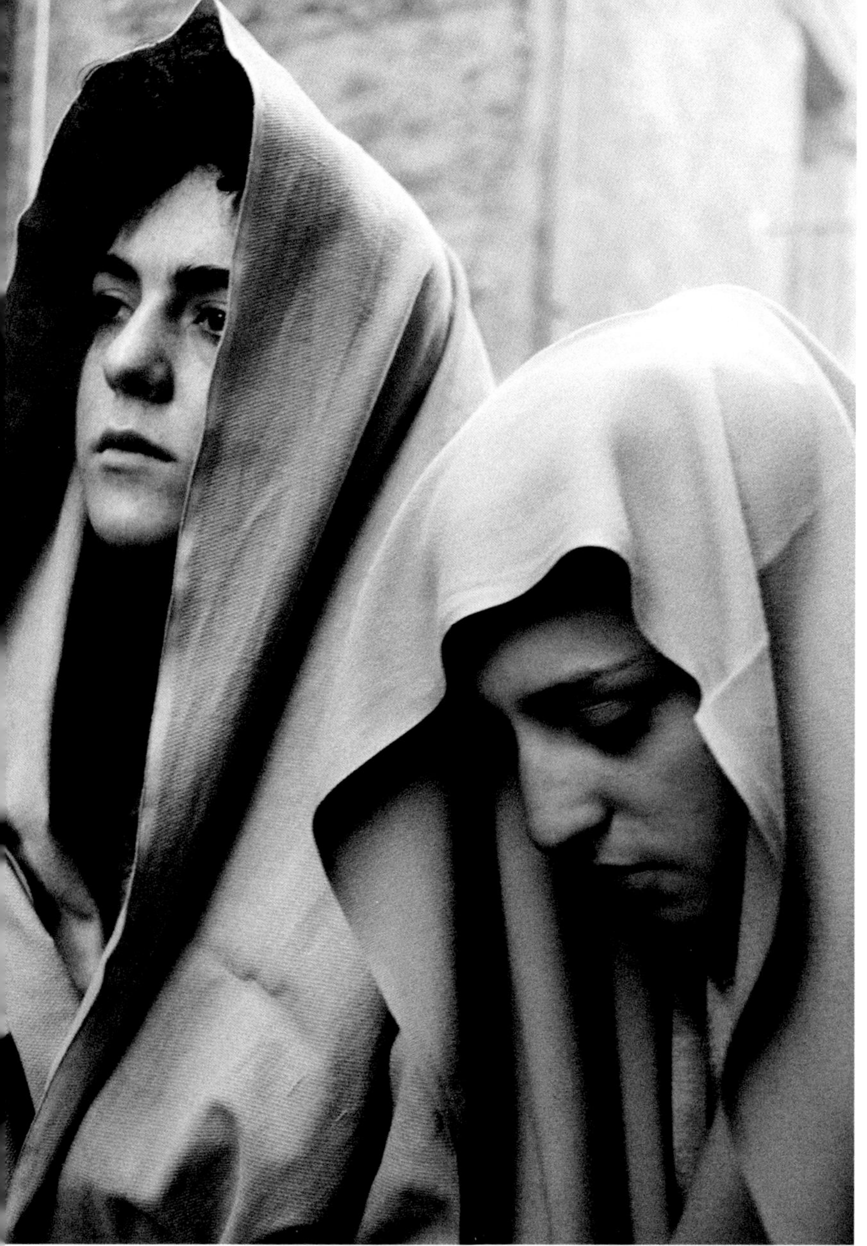

59. *Easter Sunday: The traditional race following the Resurrected Christ*, Ribera, 1984.

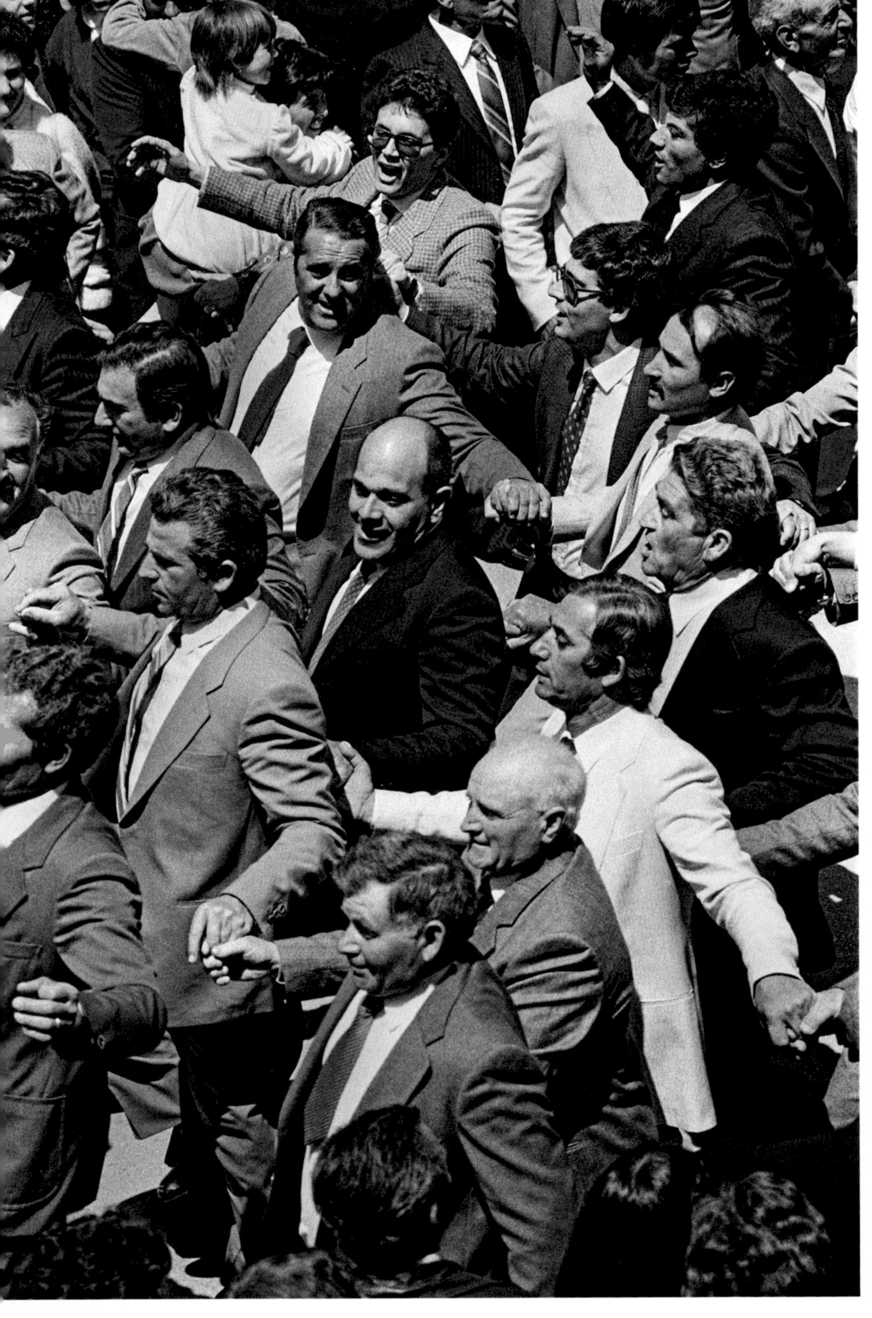

60. *Woman smoking*, Catania, 1984.

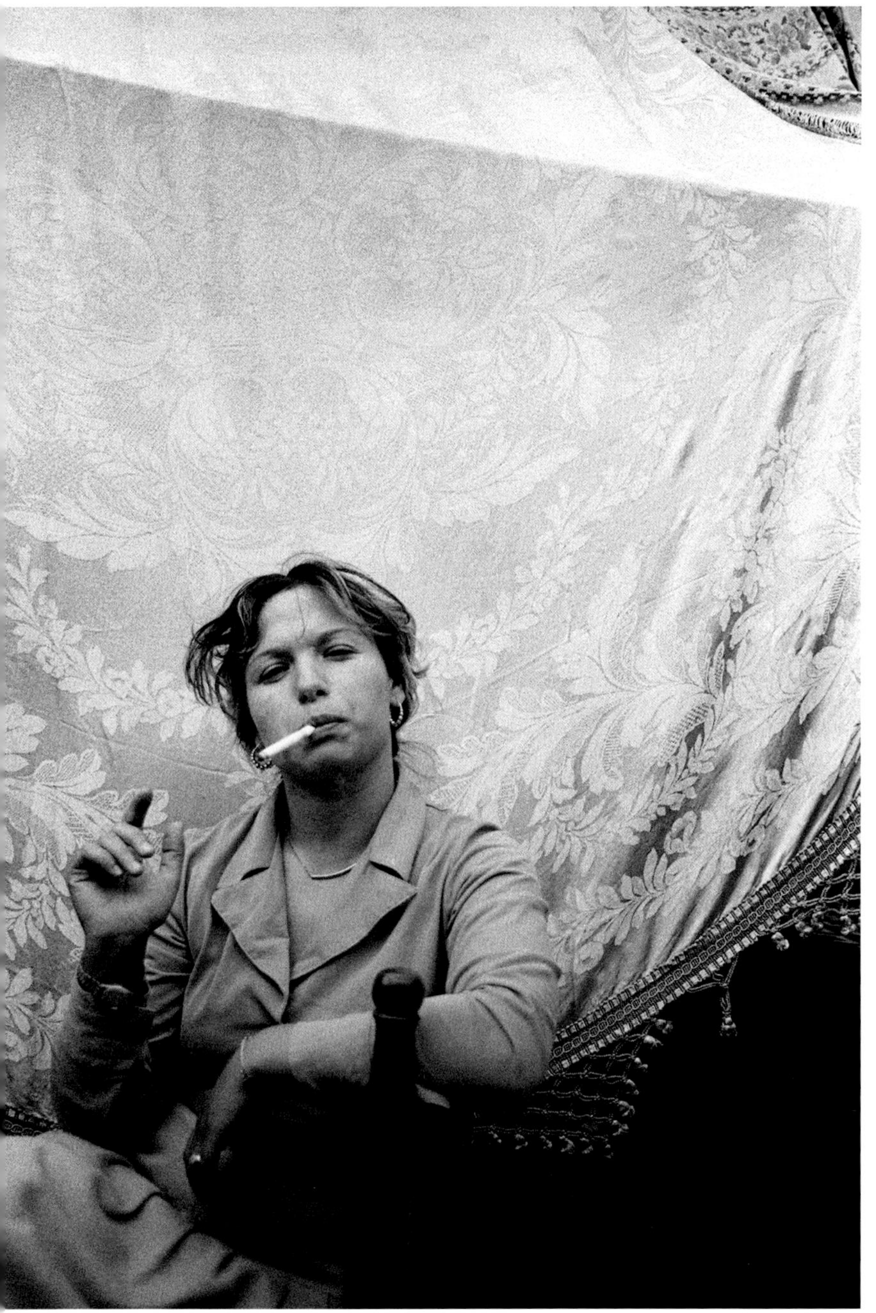

61. Moscow, USSR, 1989.

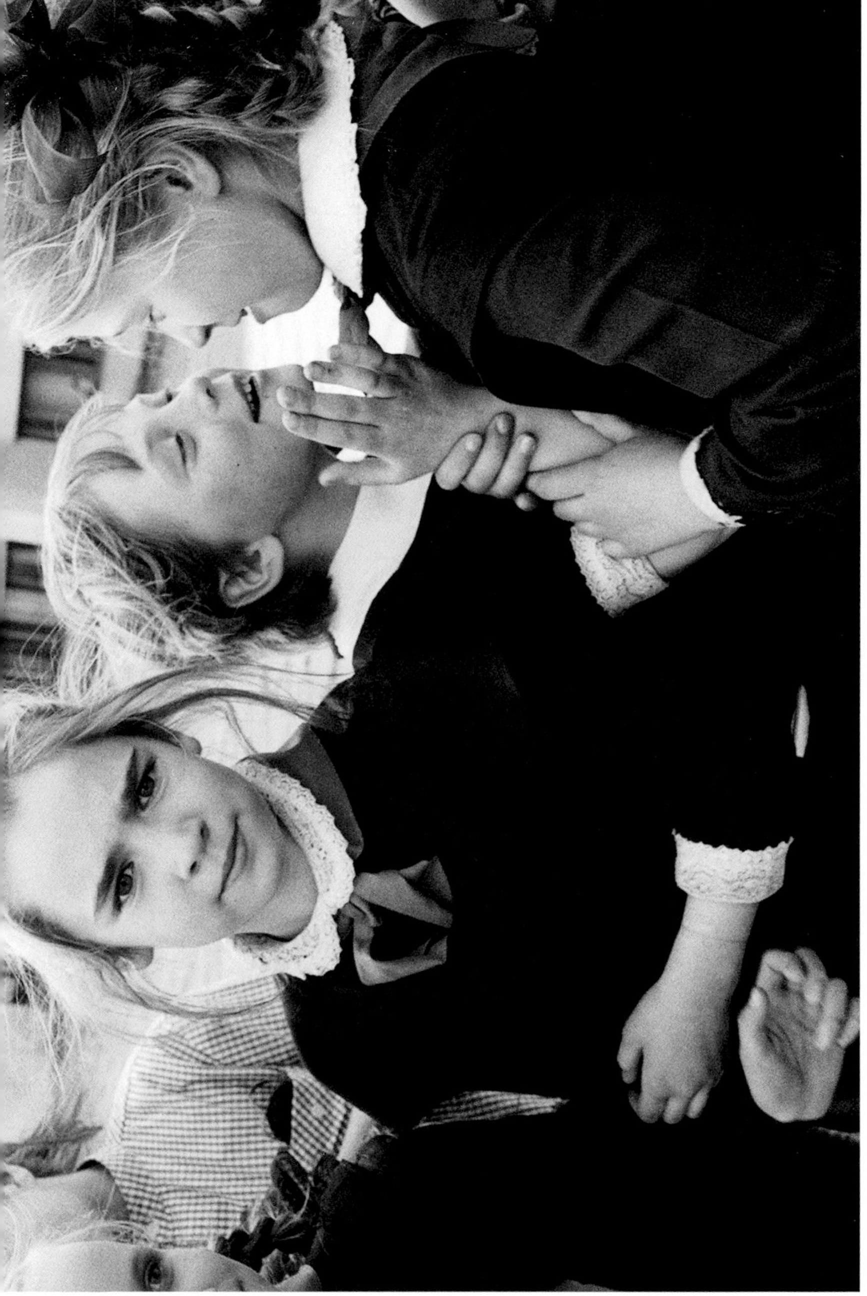

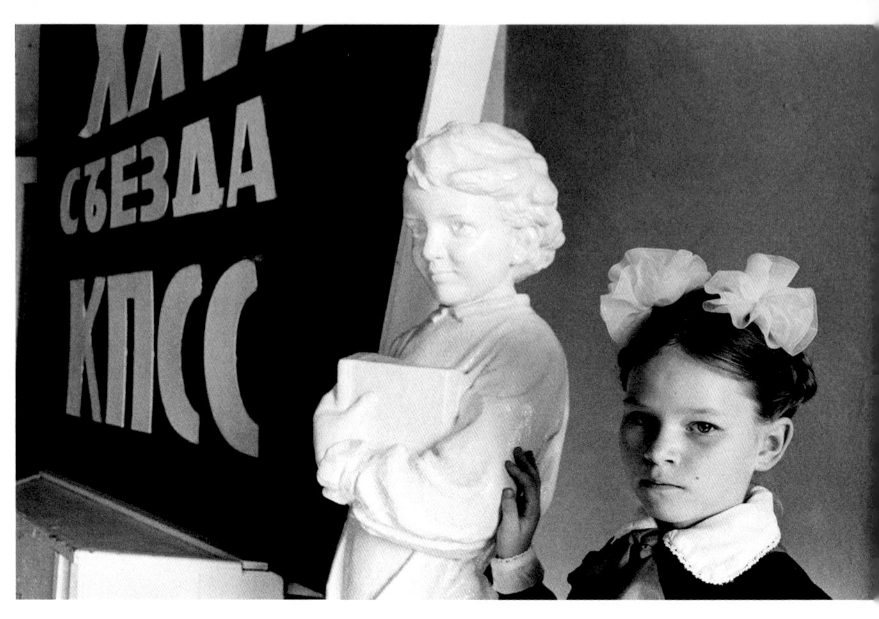

62. Moscow, USSR, 1989.

63. *Lizzie in a shelter*, New York, USA, 1985.

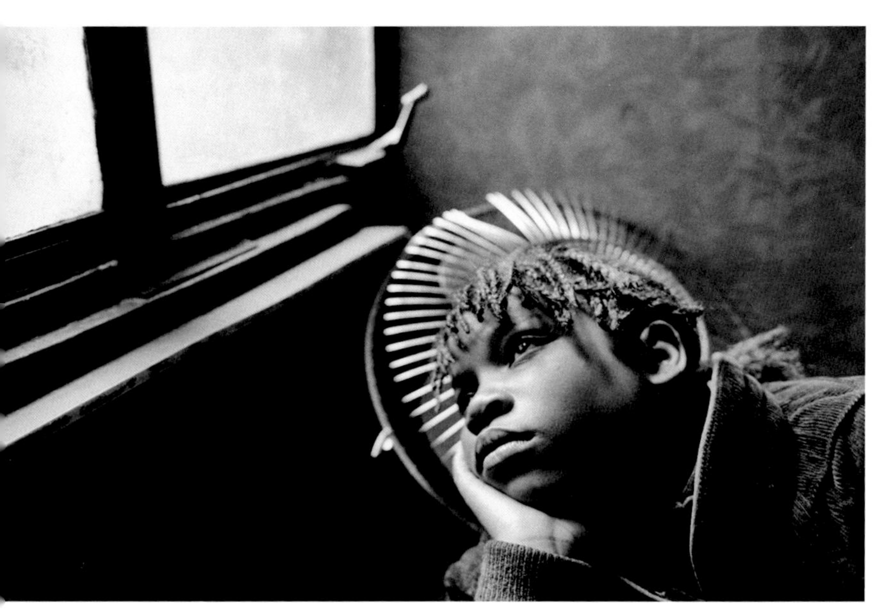

64. Greenland, 1993.

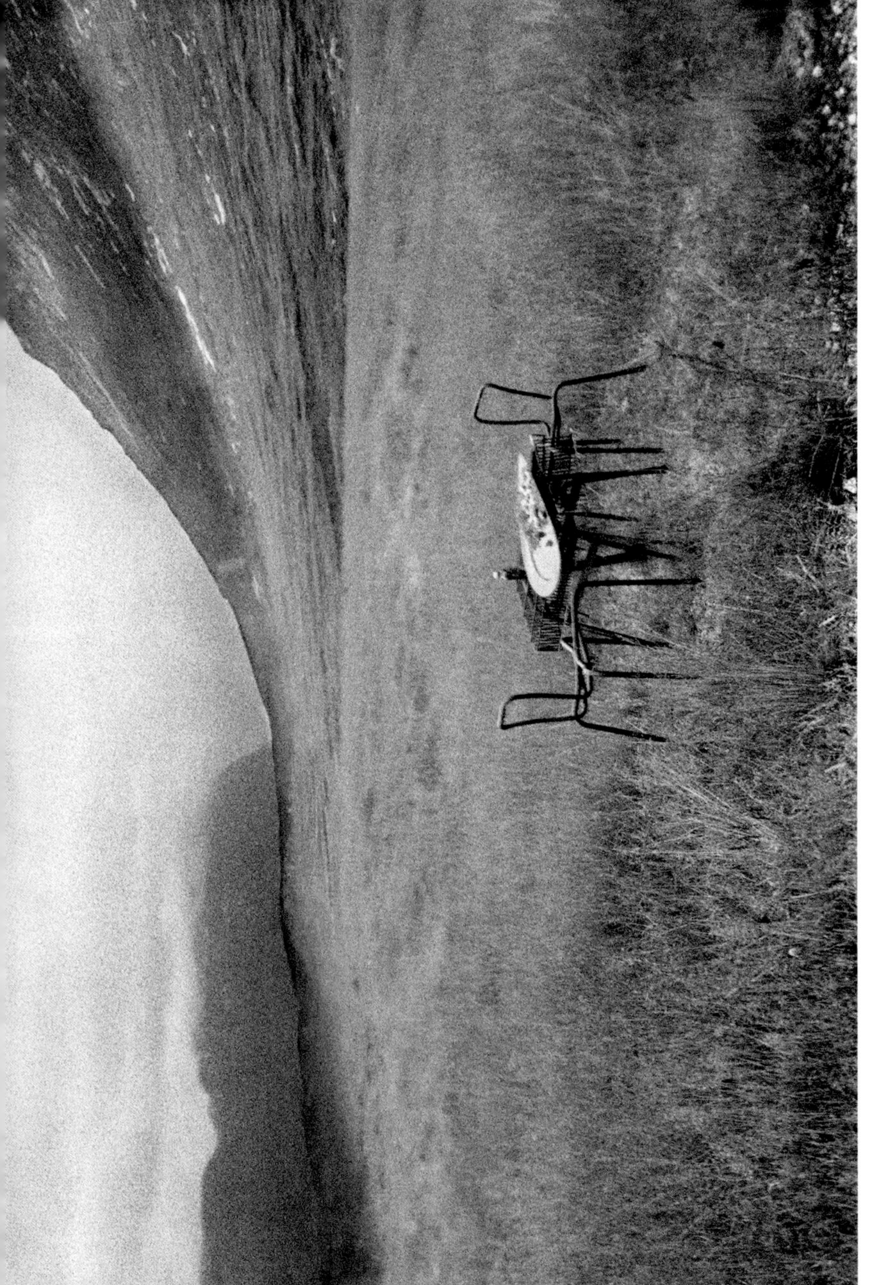

65. Yugoslavia, 1985.

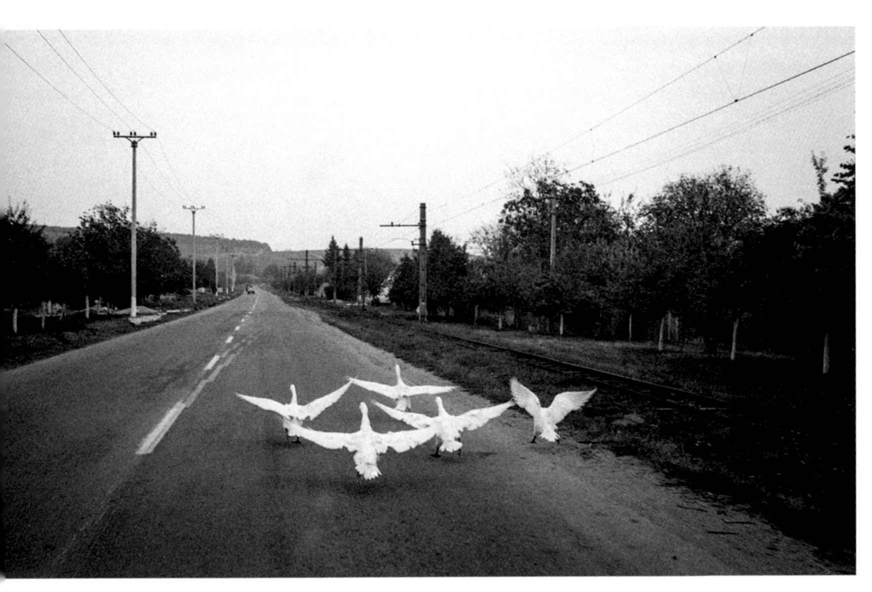

Biography

1935 Letizia Battaglia is born in Palermo, Sicily, on 5 March.

1969 Starts working as a journalist for the Palermo daily newspaper *L'Ora*. While in this role, she starts taking photographs.

1971–74 Joins the photographer Santi Caleca in Milan. Works for the weekly paper *ABC* (then edited by Ruggero Orlando), the periodical *Os*, and the magazines *Le Ore*, *Homo*, *Duepiù* and *Vie nuove*.

In 1972, she photographs Pier Paolo Pasolini at the Circolo Turati during a debate on the theme of 'Freedom of Expression through Repression and Pornography'.

In 1974, she photographs the occupation of the Palazzina Liberty by Dario Fo, Franca Rame and their theatre collective.

1974 *L'Ora* asks Letizia Battaglia and Santi Caleca to run its photography department; the two journalists return to Palermo.

1976–91 Works for the newspaper *L'Ora* with Franco Zecchin, with whom she founds the group Informazione Fotografica and the IF Laboratory. During this period, she becomes one of the main witnesses of the Mafia wars and photographs some of the bloodiest events in Italian history, including the killing of judges, police officers and politicians. Develops a special photographic sensitivity to Sicilian women, girls and young children, living in poverty-stricken conditions.

1977 As part of her anti-Mafia work, she co-founds, alongside Umberto Santino, Anna Puglisi, Franco Zecchin and others, the Centro Siciliano di Documentazione, which will later be dedicated to the memory of Giuseppe Impastato, a journalist killed by the Mafia in 1978.

1970s–80s Attends a course on directing at the theatre school Teatès, led by Michele Perriera. Organizes theatre workshops and plays at the psychiatric hospital in Palermo.

1985 Letizia Battaglia becomes, alongside Donna Ferrato, the first European woman to receive the W. Eugene Smith Grant in New York.

1986–87 Gets involved in politics, running for Palermo city council as a candidate for the Green Party. A year later, she becomes city councillor for urban livability, under the Mayor of Palermo, Leoluca Orlando.

Enters the world of publishing, founding the monthly cultural and political magazine *Grandevù: Grandezze e bassezze della città di Palermo*.

1991 Becomes a deputy at the Sicilian Regional Assembly for the party La Rete. Alongside Simona Mafai and others, she founds *Mezzocielo*, a bimonthly magazine created by and for women.

1992 Shocked and disgusted by the violent murders of judges Giovanni Falcone and Paolo Borsellino, she decides to stop photographing Mafia crimes.

Founding of the publishing house Edizioni della battaglia.

2007 Letizia Battaglia receives the Dr Erich Salomon Award from the Deutsche Gesellschaft für Photographie.

2009 Wins the Cornell Capa Infinity Award and is recommended for a Nobel Peace Prize by the organization Peace Women Across the Globe.

2017 Becomes the only Italian to appear in the *New York Times* list of the most influential women in the world. In November, she opens the Centro Internazionale di Fotografia in the Cantieri Culturali alla Zisa, in Palermo, which she runs until the end of her life.

2020–21 Tells her life story to her friend, the filmmaker Roberto Andò, who turns it into a two-part film, *Solo per passione: Letizia Battaglia fotografa*, broadcast by Italian TV channel Rai 1 in May 2022.

2021 The Archivio Letizia Battaglia is founded with the help of her grandchildren, Matteo and Marta Sollima, with the aim of promoting and preserving her work.

2022 Letizia Battaglia dies on 13 April in Palermo, surrounded by her family.

Selected Bibliography

Passion, Justice, Freedom: Photographs of Sicily, text by Alexander Stille, Renate Siebert, Roberto Scarpinato *et al*., New York: Aperture; London: Robert Hale; Arles: Actes Sud: Milan: Federico Motta, 1999

Sergio Troisi (ed.), *Due o tre cose che so di lei*, with Gaetano Cipolla, Palermo: Edizioni di Passaggio, 2008

Diario, Rome: Castelvecchi, 2014

Paolo Falcone (ed.), *Per pura passione*, Rome: Drago, 2016

Paolo Falcone (ed.), *Anthologia*, Rome: Drago, 2016

Archivi della Resistenza (ed.), *La strada, la lotta, l'amore*, with Tano D'Amico and Uliano Lucas, text by Michele Smargiassi, Pisa: ets, 2019

Francesca Alfano Miglietti (ed.), *Fotografia come scelta di vita*, Venice: Marsilio, 2019

Sabrina Pisu, *Mi prendo il mundo ovunque sia*, Turin: Einaudi, 2020

Volare alto, volare basso. Conversazioni, ricordi e invettive, with Goffredo Fofi, Rome: Contrasto, 2021

Franco Zecchin, *Letizia*, text by Roberto Andò, Rome: Postcart, 2023

Paolo Falcone & Sabrina Pisu (eds.), *Letizia Battaglia senza fine*, Milan: Electa, 2023

Paolo Falcone (ed.), *Letizia Battaglia sono io*, Rome: Contrasto, 2023

Marco Meneguzzo (ed.), *Chronique, vie, amour*, Paris: Istituto Italiano di Cultura, 2023

Franco Maresco, *La mia Battaglia. Conversazioni con Letizia Battaglia*, Milan: Il Saggiatore, 2023

Walter Guadagnini (ed.), Letizia Battaglia, Milan: Dario Cimorelli; Paris: Jeu de Paume, 2024

Paolo Falcone (ed.), *Letizia Battaglia: Life, Love and Death in Sicily*, Rome: Contrasto; London: The Photographers' Gallery, 2024

Selected Exhibitions

Solo exhibitions

1983 *Nobili, signori e disgraziati*, Galleria San Fedele, Milan.

1985 Festival de la Photographie, Lausanne.
Prima di essere donna, Cinema Metropolitan, Palermo.

1999 *La Mafia sicilienne*, Visa pour l'Image, Perpignan.

2000 XpoSeptember, Stockholm Foto Festival.
Huis Marseille, Amsterdam.
National Geographic, Washington DC.

2001 School of Visual Arts, New York.
Passion, Justice, Freedom, Burden Gallery, New York.

2006 *Passione, giustizia, libertà*, San Giuseppe al Duomo, Catania.

2007 Ernst Bloch Zentrum, Ludwigshafen; Akademie der Künste, Berlin.
Sicilia en Blanco y Negro, Cinemateca Uruguaya, Montevideo.

2009 *Quando la guerra è civile*, Università di Pavia.
Kunsthaus Nürnberg, Nuremberg.
Una vita contro la mafia, Palazzo dei Sette, Orvieto.

2010–11 *Vintages 1972–1993*, S.T. foto libreria galleria, Rome.

2011 *Opere siciliane*, Gratteri.
Galleria Comunale, FotoArte, Tarento.
Letizia Battaglia 1974–2011, Palazzo Chiaramonte Steri, Palermo.

2013 Galerie Cardi, Artissima, Lingotto Fiere, Turin.

2014 *Gli invincibili*, Nonostante Marras, Milan.
Breaking the Code of Silence, Open Eye Gallery, Liverpool.

2015 *Rompere il muro del silenzio*, Fondazione Mazzullo, Taobuk, Taormina.
Qualcosa di mio, Ex Stabilimento Florio delle Tonnare di Favignana e Formica, Favignana; Museo Civico, Castelbuono.
Letizia Battaglia 1974–2015, Palazzo della Ragione, Domina Domna, Bergamo.

2016 ManifestO, Toulouse.
Anthologia, ZAC, Palermo.

2016–17 *Per pura passione*, maxxi, Rome.

2019 *Fotografia come scelta di vita*, Casa dei Tre Oci, Venice.
Museo Civico Giovanni Fattori, Livorno.
Palermo, Instituto Morreira-Salles, São Paulo; Rio de Janeiro.

2019–21 *Storie di strada*, Palazzo Reale, Milan; Mole Vanvitelliana, Ancona.

2020 *Minime d'amore*, FPAC, Palermo.
Corpo di donna, Crumb Gallery, Florence.

2022 *Vintage Prints*, Galleria del Cembalo, Rome.
Photography as a Life Choice, Galerija Jakopič, Ljubljana.

2023 *Letizia Battaglia. Storie di libertà ritrovata*, LCA Studio Legale, Milan.
Letizia Battaglia. Sono io, Palazzo Ducale, Genoa.

2023–24 *Letizia Battaglia: Senza fine*, Terme di Caracalla, Rome; Area Megalitica, Aosta; Arena dello Stretto, Reggio de Calabria.
Letizia Battaglia: Chronique, vie, amour, Istituto Italiano di Cultura, Paris; Istituto Italiano di Cultura, Brussels; Sala TAC, Caracas; Museo Provincial de Fotografía Palacio Dionisi, Córdoba; Centro Cultural Recoleta, Buenos Aires; MAC Parque Forestal, Santiago de Chile.

2024–25 *Letizia Battaglia: Life, Love and Death in Sicily*, The Photographers' Gallery, London.

2024–26 *Letizia Battaglia*, Jeu de Paume, Château de Tours; Rencontres d'Arles; Camera, Turin.

Group exhibitions

1979 *Mafia oggi*, Centro Siciliano di Documentazione, Palermo.
Via Pindemonte e dintorni, Pietro Pisani Psychiatric Hospital, Palermo.

1981 *L'informazione negata. Il fotogiornalismo in Italia, 1945/1980*, Pinacoteca Corrado Giaquinto, Bari.

1982 *Reporter a Milano 1968–1982*, Palazzo Dugnani, Milan.

1983 *The Sicilian Mafia*, Camerawork, London;
Istituto Italiano di Cultura, Amsterdam.

1984 *Güzel. Un viaggio in Turchia*, Galerie
Il Diaframma, Milan.

1986 *Letizia Battaglia / Franco Zecchin*,
George Eastman House, Rochester, NY.

1989 *Chroniques siciliennes*, Centre National
de la Photographie, Paris; Photovision,
Montpellier.

1990 FotoFest, Houston, Texas.
Galerie Municipale du Château d'Eau,
Toulouse.

1991 *Le Mythe de W. Eugene Smith:
12 photographes héritiers d'une tradition
humaniste*, Centre Pompidou, Paris.

1992 Musée de l'Élysée, Lausanne.

1993 *Fictions vraies*, Istituto Italiano
di Cultura, Paris.
Il fotogiornalismo oggi in Italia,
Palazzo Alberti Poja, Rovereto.

1993–94 *Immagini italiane*, Peggy
Guggenheim Collection, Venice; Museo
Diego Aragona Pignatelli Cortes, Naples;
The Murray and Isabella Rayburn Foundation,
New York.

1995 *L'io e il suo doppio. Un secolo di ritratto
fotografico in Italia, 1895–1995*, Italian
Pavilion, Venice Biennale; Museo di Storia
della Fotografia Fratelli Alinari, Florence.

2003 *Women Photographers: European
Experiences*, Hasselblad Center, Gothenburg.

2005–6 *Il fotogiornalismo in Italia 1945–2005*,
Palazzo Bricherasio, Turin; Museo Civico di
Storia Contemporanea, Milan.

2006 *Closed Eyes*, Kunsthallen Brandts
Museet for Fotokunst, Odense.
Dovere di cronaca, Istituto Nazionale per
la Grafica, Festival FotoGrafia, Rome.

2008–10 *Italics. Arte italiana fra tradizione
e rivoluzione, 1968–2008*, Palazzo Grassi,
Venice; Museum of Contemporary Art,
Chicago.

2009 *Background Story*, Galerie Cardi, Milan.

2010 *Disquieting Images*, Triennale, Milan.
*Exposed: Voyeurism, Surveillance and
the Camera*, Tate Modern, London.

2011 *Mafia(s)*, Chais des Moulins, Images
Singulières, Sète.
Untitled, Istanbul Biennial.

2011–12 *La nuova scuola di fotografia siciliana*,
Galleria Credito Siciliano, Acireale; Galleria
Gruppo Credito Valtellinese, Milan.

2012 *Giovanni Falcone, eroe italiano*,
Italian Embassy, Washington DC.
Letizia Battaglia / Francesca Woodman,
Galerie Massimo Minini, Brescia.

2013 *Antimafia*, Arsenal Jean-Marie-Rausch,
Metz.

2015 *Italia Inside Out*, Palazzo della Ragione,
Milan.

2016–17 *L'altro sguardo. Fotografie Italiane
1965–2015*, Triennale, Milan.

2016 *Gangcity*, Spazio Thetis, Venice Biennale.

2018 *L'altro sguardo. Fotografe Italiane
1965–2018*, Palazzo delle Esposizioni, Rome.

2018–19 *La condizione umana. Oltre
l'istituzione totale*, Palazzo Ajutamicristo,
Palermo.

2019 *Quelli de L'Ora. Dal 1974*, Centro
Internazionale di Fotografia, Palermo.

2022 *Essere umane. Le grandi fotografe
raccontano il mondo*, Musei San Domenico,
Forlì.

2023 *Palermo mon amour*, Fondazione Merz,
Turin; Istituto Italiano di Cultura, Madrid.

The Photofile series is the original English-language edition of the Photo Poche collection. It was first published between 1986 and 1992 by the Centre National de la Photographie, Paris, with the support of the French Ministry of Culture. Robert Delpire (1926–2017) was the creator of the series and its managing editor until 2017.

Series design by Matthew Young

General editor: Géraldine Lay

Introduction translated from the Italian by Emma Mandley

First published in the United Kingdom in 2026 by
Thames & Hudson Ltd, 6–24 Britannia Street, London WC1X 9JD

First published in 2026 in the United States of America by
Thames & Hudson Inc., 500 Fifth Avenue, New York, New York 10110

EU Authorized Representative: Interart S.A.R.L.
19 rue Charles Auray, 93500 Pantin, Paris, France
productsafety@thameshudson.co.uk
www.interart.fr

A CIP catalogue record for this book is available from the British Library

Library of Congress Catalog Card Number 2025936036

ISBN 978-0-500-41131-5
01

Printed and bound in Italy

Be the first to know about our new releases,
exclusive content and author events by visiting
thamesandhudson.com
thamesandhudsonusa.com
thamesandhudson.com.au